ACCIDENTAL WILDERNESS

ACCIDENTAL WILDERNESS

The Origins and Ecology of Toronto's Tommy Thompson Park

Walter H. Kehm with photographs by Robert Burley

Aevo UTP
An imprint of University of Toronto Press
Toronto Buffalo London
utorontopress.com

**Library and Archives Canada Cataloguing in
Publication**

Title: Accidental wilderness : the origins and
  ecology of Toronto's Tommy Thompson Park /
  Walter H. Kehm ; with photographs by Robert
  Burley.
Names: Kehm, Walter H., 1937– author. | Burley,
  Robert, 1957– photographer.
Description: Includes bibliographical references
Identifiers: Canadiana (print) 20200307509
  | Canadiana (ebook) 20200308750 | ISBN
  9781487508340 (hardcover) | ISBN 9781487538057
  (EPUB) | ISBN 9781487538040 (PDF)
Subjects: LCSH: Parks – Ontario – Toronto. | LCSH:
  Parks – Ontario – Toronto – Pictorial works. | LCSH:
  Natural history – Ontario – Toronto. | LCSH: Urban
  ecology (Biology) – Ontario – Toronto. | LCSH:
  Peninsulas – Ontario – Toronto.
Classification: LCC QH106.2.O6 K44 2020 | DDC
  508.713/541 – dc23

ISBN 978-1-4875-0834-0 (cloth)
ISBN 978-1-4875-3805-7 (EPUB)
ISBN 978-1-4875-3804-0 (PDF)

Printed in Canada

Acquisitions Editor: Jodi Lewchuk
Managing Editor: Robin Studniberg
Production Manager: Ani Deyirmenjian
Copy Editing: Ashley Rayner
Proofreading: Leanne Rancourt

Project Manager: Claire Harvie
Design and Cover: Cecilia Berkovic
Imaging: Bahar Kamali

Accidental Wilderness was made possible
by the generous financial support of Mary and
Jim Connacher and family, Ryerson University, and
the Ontario Association of Landscape Architects.

We acknowledge the financial support of the
Government of Canada, the Canada Council for
the Arts, and the Ontario Arts Council, an agency
of the Government of Ontario, for our publishing
activities.

Recognition, Respect, and Relationships

This book is an acknowledgement of the enduring presence of Indigenous peoples who have inhabited these lands and waters for over 10,000 years. We pay tribute to their teachings about the sacred earth upon which all life is dependent. We have been given the gifts of clean air and water, abundant vegetation, and diverse fish, animals, and insects. Within nature are the seeds of regeneration that allow the cycle of life to continue. As we seek reconciliation with Indigenous peoples, we are aware of the need to recognize the sanctity of the earth and its people and pay tribute to it as our home and refuge.

The authors offer this book as a tribute to all the unsung champions of "The Spit" who have worked tirelessly over many decades to protect and preserve this unique landscape. Their stewardship continues to this day, sustaining the diverse biological character of this urban wilderness for others to enjoy.

This book is dedicated to my family, who have supported and shared in my lifelong obsession with the natural world.

— WALTER H. KEHM

Contents

Foreword
David Miller — xi

Introduction
Walter H. Kehm — 1

PORTFOLIO I
Robert Burley — 5

PART I: EPIPHANY

**The Spontaneous Ecology
of Tommy Thompson Park**
Peter Del Tredici — 31

Building the Leslie Street Spit
Wayne Reeves — 35

Aquatic Park
Walter H. Kehm — 43

The Evolution of Advocacy
John Carley — 49

PORTFOLIO II
Robert Burley — 55

PART II: PROCESS

**Conservation by Design:
The 1986 Plan**
Walter H. Kehm — 85

Plants and Natural Succession
Gavin Miller — 99

Birds and Birding at the Spit
Garth Vernon Riley — 109

Mammals and Fish
*Gord MacPherson
and Walter H. Kehm* — 115

**Habitat Projects and
Wildlife Management**
Andrea Chreston — 119

PORTFOLIO III
Robert Burley — 123

PART III: EVOLUTION

People in the Park
Walter H. Kehm — 153

Let the Spit Be!!
Robert Burley — 157

Home
Chief R. Stacey Laforme — 161

Acknowledgments — 163
Comparative Parks — 164
List of Bird Species — 165
List of Plant Species — 169
References — 175
Further Resources — 177
Image Key — 178
Contributors — 180

Foreword

David Miller

About a dozen years ago, on a searingly hot July day, I rode my bike from High Park in the city's west end to the Leslie Street Spit in the east. The Spit was a place I knew well, and it was a good destination for a retreat on a rare free Saturday afternoon. I arrived at the Spit hot and sweaty, and it seemed the most natural thing in the world to dive into Lake Ontario for a swim.

When I wanted to get out, I realized that I had created a significant problem for myself. The Spit is made of waste deliberately dumped into Lake Ontario to create a protective point of land – primarily, this waste is the debris of demolished buildings and the dirt removed to make room for the basements of Toronto's tallest towers. Swimming at the Spit means climbing over rebar, concrete slabs, and other construction waste on the shore, neither easy nor safe. And certainly not elegant, as I climbed through what seemed like a small forest of rusting iron rods to get out of the clean but cold waters of Lake Ontario. If it were today, there would certainly be amusing videos on social media of Toronto's then Chief Magistrate struggling awkwardly to get out of the water, at a place where swimming was no doubt banned.

Construction debris, concrete, old pieces of reinforcing material – these are part of the essence of the Leslie Street Spit. Designed as a cheap way to dispose of waste from the building boom of the late 1950s and early 60s, the Spit in my eyes had always been simply the place where rubble was dumped to allow for the building of Toronto's downtown skyscrapers. Although this is true, the reality is much more complex. As this important and passionate book makes clear, failed plans for a port expansion, the needs of Toronto's development industry, visionary public servants, and activist citizens are all part of the history of the Spit – in other words, the core forces of Toronto's typical municipal political scene came together to create this human-built landform.

But, with one other profound influence: nature. The Spit, of course, though originally a dumping ground, has become an incredible nature reserve because nature chose the Spit. We, as humans, have helped, but mostly by getting out of the way: sometimes by accident while there were debates about plans, but later deliberately as the result of strong activist intervention by citizens who understood the remarkable transformation that was happening literally in front of our eyes.

I've been going to the Spit for 40 years and have seen nature's transformation first hand. A couple of years ago, my wife, Jill, and I walked with our dog Jimmy from Cherry Beach to the Spit across a frozen lake. The Spit was simply beautiful in its winter state, with the sun glistening from icy trees (also beautiful was the view of the Toronto skyline from the Spit). This book lovingly explains the forces and actions that helped this miracle come about – and documents it with especially superb photography. It's a fitting tribute to a place built on human-created waste that nature has taken back as its own.

David Miller
Mayor of Toronto, 2003–10
July 2020

Tommy Thompson Park
Aerial Photo, 2013. (TRCA)

Introduction

Walter H. Kehm

This wasn't meant to be.

On a cloudless, blue-sky day in January 1986, I took a bike ride into the park. I pedalled through low grasses, past 20-foot tall trees, and alongside a series of open ponds where hundreds, if not thousands, of Bufflehead and Scaup ducks were floating and diving peacefully. The gulls of various species at the ponds were just as numerous. Every glance I took composed itself into a kind of photograph, different from the last but a seamless part of a growing album.

Just past the ponds, though, I caught sight of something that didn't seem to fit: a large, white object in the branches of a tree in the distance ahead of me. I thought at first that it was a plastic bag. Plastic, after all, is everywhere; it's modern humanity's fate. But as I got closer, the bag in question became something else: motionless, quiet, statuesque, and alive. It was a Snowy Owl, an Arctic bird most commonly seen in the vast tundra 2,000 kilometres north of where I sat astride my bike. I dismounted carefully and approached the tree, step by gradual step; the owl paid no attention to me. I stopped three metres away. Suddenly, its head swivelled in that magical way an owl's head will, so it could regard me.

The owl and I were looking at each other in a city park ten minutes away from downtown Toronto, on a man-made isthmus, a spit of land jutting five-and-a-half kilometres into Lake Ontario from the foot of Leslie Street. The park is known officially as Tommy Thompson Park, named for a visionary former Toronto Parks Commissioner, but it was known more commonly as the

Leslie Street Spit. It was also already being called the "Everglades of the North," a world-recognized site for bird-watching and the observation in microcosm of the natural succession of plants, fish, amphibians, insects, and mammals.

But here's the thing: The Park, the Spit, the Everglades of the North was built almost entirely of dredged sand and urban rubble. And it was a complete accident.

* * *

In the late 1950s the Toronto Harbour Commission embarked on the construction of an ambitious landfill project that would serve as a breakwater for a new Outer Harbour for the city's waterfront. The impetus was the Saint Lawrence Seaway, due to be opened in 1959. At that point, the thinking ran, Great Lakes shipping traffic would surge, and Toronto would need extended harbour capacity to accommodate the dramatically greater number of ships that would pass through the Great Lakes system. What no one predicted, though, was the "containerization" revolution of the 1960s, which meant most sea-going goods were now loaded in uniform containers perfectly sized for truck rigs and trains. The sea cargo traffic put in at East Coast ports and Montreal instead, cutting ship arrivals in Toronto in half. A shipping-ready Outer Harbour was never needed.

I arrived in Toronto in 1965. By the fall of 1986 I would be working with a landscape architecture firm I had co-founded, E.D.A. Collaborative, Inc., and completed several

Fig. 1

Aerial view, looking westward, of lakefilling to create "the Flats," 1986. (TRCA)

Fig. 2

Fig. 2
Snowy Owl, 2018 (TRCA)

major park-planning and design projects. But because of a particular passion and pastime of mine, I was also witness to the creation of the Leslie Street landfill spit in the 1970s, as construction continued even after the original *modus vivendi* of the project had disappeared. I'd grown up in New York City next to Idlewild Airport, which would become John F. Kennedy International Airport. My brother and I were both in the Boy Scouts, and we did wetland bird-watching near Idlewild on a regular basis. In Toronto, to satisfy my habit, I gravitated to the Spit and Cherry Beach, in the eastern harbour, which was a bird-watching magnet in its own right. Later I started rowing in the area at the Hanlan Boat Club. If I wasn't bird-watching near the Spit, chances were good I was up at 6:00 a.m. rowing around it and into its embayments and cells.

It was, initially, as barren a place as you could imagine. It was a construction site. Bulldozers were moving dirt everywhere, and trucks were arriving in a steady vanguard, 300 to 400 trucks a day, carrying landfill, almost all of it demolition rubble from other construction sites in the city and beyond. Rubble from the Yonge and Bloor subway lines' construction

was an early contributor, then commercial buildings and most notably the St. James Town housing project, which required the razing of blocks of 1880s Victorian brick buildings along Parliament Street. The process was like reverse archeology: Instead of digging to discover its lost neighbourhoods, Toronto was knocking its neighbourhoods down, and then sinking them in the lake to form a bedrock for an "Aquatic Park," the now-official designation of the future Spit in the new plan Metropolitan Toronto and Region Conservation Authority (MTRCA, now TRCA) had devised for it. As the Aquatic Park plan was developing, other proponents suggested soccer fields, marinas for 1,000 boats, an amusement theme park, a rowing course, a historic boat museum, and an aquarium. The possibility of moving the Island Airport (the current Billy Bishop Airport) to the Spit was also entertained; a Toronto Harbour Master Plan was created with this prospect. The lands occupied by the airport were envisioned as a massive "Venice-of-the-North" housing and mixed-use development.

Not surprisingly, given the times, MTRCA's plan developed three zones, including Natural Resource, Recreation, and Long-Term Development options. It didn't matter. As the cavalcade of trucks kept coming at a dizzying rate, bringing tons of debris, something else was starting to happen that transcended reverse archeology. Nature was reclaiming the rubble. Whether it was concrete blocks or bricks or broken pavement or rebar or the aggregates that were mined in the surrounding countryside or dredgeate from lake channels, it was all coming back to the Spit. Sand from the moraines had once been collected for silicate, which was used to make glass for the windows in the Victorian homes, while clay from the Don Valley Brickworks had been mined for buildings that now were being demolished. The resulting debris was randomly dumped on the Spit, where wave action and erosion turned it back into sand, silt, and clay. It's a standard trope in our human-centric world that people despoil nature: Nature creates paradise, and we ruin it. But in this case people had created a wasteland, and nature was rescuing it. Ironically, some of the credit was ours; we played a part in the cycle of birth, death, and rebirth. Through destruction and all its guises, demolitions and disintegrations, we had inadvertently created a new mechanism for the renewal of a healthy city.

The grasses came first, some time in the early '70s. The trees began appearing in the late '70s and early '80s. When I first started going to the Spit, the trees were 15 feet high. By this point the birds were there, too, the Caspian Terns and the thousands of Ring-billed Gulls, all coming back to the city. I remember thinking to myself: How is this happening on this wasteland, this abundance of vegetation and life? How all of *this*, from those truckloads of rubble? It was like a Rube Goldberg version of the glacier that, a hundred thousand years ago at the time of the last ice age, had started moving south on the continent like a giant snowplow, picking up detritus on its way from the Arctic down to Lake Iroquois, and then dumping its erratic stones and boulders and eskers and whole river valleys wherever nature told it to. Now, instead of the glacier, we had the bulldozer. It took whatever we piled on it and dumped it wherever we told it to. True, a bulldozer is a lot smaller than a glacier, but we lived in an age of nanotechnology. In the nano age, the dump truck was a mini-truck. And the glacier was Tepperman's Wrecking Company.

Fortunately, the Friends of the Spit, a local activist group, rejected the Aquatic Park Plan, and public criticism of the Recreation and Long-Term Development plans reached a fever pitch. The general message? *Leave the Spit alone*. MTRCA decided to let the private sector take the heat. They put out a proposal to landscape architectural firms to submit a new plan for the Spit, a bio-sanctuary as opposed to a typical park or activity area. Ours was one of the firms that made a submission. We were awarded the commission in 1986.

Two months later I stood beside my fallen bicycle, locking gazes with a Snowy Owl. Among other things, I remember thinking at that moment about the universe; but the universal is never very far from the personal. As a child growing up in New York City I had been most awed not by the height of skyscrapers but by the sight of a green shoot growing in sidewalk concrete expansion joints I walked over. Then I saw a Tree of Heaven (*Ailanthus altissima*) growing between my public-school foundation and the asphalt. This phenomenon also puzzled me, and I remember discussing this with my mother. Her German background was rural and her family farmers. She had a passion for all things green and in nature, and it is from her that I received a unique indoctrination about plants and from, of all places, the city. How is it possible, that this green should grow from a pavement crack? As the German expression goes: *Wie funkioniert das?* How does this function? And why was I so fascinated by it, enough that I took the Garden Science stream in high school? Who took Garden Science, for that matter, in a New York City high school? What was it all for?

Standing in Tommy Thompson Park, sharing a stare with a majestic Snowy Owl, I finally knew.

It was for this.

PORTFOLIO I

1
View of Lake Ontario from
the Endikement, 2019

2
Shoreline of the Flats
with brick and rebar
constructions, 2020

3
Cyclists on the shoreline
of the Endikement, 2019

above

4
Brick and concrete
building remnants,
the Endikement, 2020

opposite page

5
Constructions of brick
and rebar, Lighthouse
Point, 2019

following pages

6
Cottonwood tree in
rubble landform on the
Endikement, 2019

7
Quaking Aspen trees
with metal parts, the
Endikement, 2019

8
Hawthorn tree on the tip
of the Endikement, 2020

9
Wildflowers in
the Flats, 2014

following pages

10
Landform in the
Toplands, 2020

11
Meadow in the
Toplands, 2020

12
View of Toronto skyline
from Lighthouse Point, 2019

previous page

13
Lighthouse Point, 2020

opposite page

14
Jogger at Cell 3, 2014

PART I: EPIPHANY

The Spontaneous Ecology of Tommy Thompson Park

Peter Del Tredici

One of the most important ideas underlying modern evolutionary biology is that elemental matter, when exposed to the proper environmental conditions, can spontaneously organize itself into the basic building blocks of life – amino acids and nucleotides. With time these compounds will combine to form larger, more complex molecules – proteins and nucleic acids – that make all life possible. By analogy, when a diverse array of living organisms come together under the right environmental conditions, they will spontaneously organize themselves into ecologically functional associations that are adapted to local conditions.

In light of the world's current climate crisis, this eco-evolutionary perspective on how ecosystems form provides a basis for optimism, because it suggests that nature is more resilient than people typically give it credit for. Nothing exemplifies this resilience better than Toronto's Tommy Thompson Park, a five-kilometre-long appendix of urban rubble jutting out into Lake Ontario. Started as a speculative landfilling project in the 1950s, construction of the so-called Leslie Street Spit was halted in the late 1970s when shifts in the shipping routes on the Great Lakes rendered it economically untenable.

Before an alternative use for the site could be agreed upon by the City – including glossy plans for an Aquatic Park – a diversity of plant seeds carried by both birds and wind began growing spontaneously on the rubble. These, in turn, were followed by a number of bird species that used the site for their summer nesting. As chance would have it, the Spit was perfect for birds, positioned as it was along two of North America's great flyways and surrounded by an abundance of fish that inhabited the adjacent, nutrient-rich waters. From the birds' perspective, it was a great place to rest, feed, and breed. From the human perspective, especially those who cared about wildlife conservation, the avian squatters and their botanical enablers had miraculously transformed a speculative rubble dump into an unexpected wildlife sanctuary (Fig. 3).

With persistent prodding from community activists, the Spit became part of Metropolitan Toronto and Region Conservation Authority (MTRCA, now TRCA) in 1982, a move that laid the groundwork for the site's protection. In the late '80s and

Fig. 3

Fig. 3

Fall-blooming seaside goldenrod (*Solidago sempervirens*) emerging in the middle of a paved road.
(Peter Del Tredici)

Fig. 4

Fig. 5

Fig. 4

Mature cottonwoods (*Populus deltoides*) line the bike path. (Peter Del Tredici)

Fig. 5

Great water dock (*Rumex britannica*) at the water's edge beneath the cormorant nests. (Peter Del Tredici)

early '90s, a thoughtful planning and design process formally transformed the Spit into a park – Tommy Thompson Park. It was a bold move because it was done, first and foremost, with the welfare of the wildlife rather than people in mind (Fig. 4). The design of the park involved three principles: 1) building a network of walking and biking paths so that people would have access to the site; 2) creating a mounded topography in order to promote habitat and wildlife diversity; and 3) reconfiguring "cells" that had been used for filling with dredge material from the harbour into biologically productive wetlands. The basic strategy was to increase access to the site for people and habitat diversity for wildlife without disrupting the existing ecology.

The take-home lesson from today's Tommy Thompson Park is crystal clear: Nature, when left to its own devices, can take care of itself. People set the table for future ecological change, but nature controlled the guest list that now consists of some 380 species of birds – a huge number that has earned the park national recognition as an "Important Bird Area." This is not to say that the ecological community in Tommy Thompson Park is to everyone's liking. The 14,000-plus pairs of Double-crested Cormorants that began arriving in the 1990s created a miniature version of the guano islands off the coast of Peru that once supplied much of the world with nitrate-rich fertilizer.

Unfortunately, the copious amounts of cormorant excrement in the park has killed many of the large eastern cottonwoods (*Populus deltoides*) that once dominated the site. While the skeletons of the dead trees still serve as nesting sites for the birds, a thick understory of herbaceous species that can tolerate the high levels of soil nitrogen has replaced them, including lamb's quarters, common mallow, great water dock, and stinging nettle (Fig. 5). Over time, the legacy of guano, both on the land and in the water, will facilitate the future development of an ecosystem that will look very different from the one that's there today. While some people may be upset that the cottonwoods are dead, that the rookery stinks to high heaven, or that the cormorants are eating too many fish, any privileging of one species over another based on a human-centric perspective would be a violation of the "Let It Be" approach that created the park's ecology in the first place.

I have no idea how many of Toronto's human inhabitants have visited Tommy Thompson Park over the past few years or how many of them appreciate how unique a landscape it is, but as an urban ecologist who has travelled the world studying the vegetation of cities – from Boston to Detroit to Berlin – I can say without hesitation that the park is a globally significant example of nature's ability to transform a landfill of waste into a functional ecological habitat – a silk purse out of a sow's ear, if you will. The success of Tommy Thompson Park, however, comes with one important caveat, namely that it takes time for nature to do its work. Ecosystems are not designed in air-conditioned downtown offices; rather, they develop slowly in response to changing environmental conditions. Engineers and designers can create a frame for ecology, but only nature – with its infinite capacity for adaptation – can provide the complexity and diversity that make it function.

One important characteristic of Tommy Thompson Park – as well as every other spontaneous urban landscape I've ever seen – is the cosmopolitan nature of its flora and fauna. The organisms that currently inhabit the site have come from the temperate regions of Asia, Europe, and North America, brought together by the same globalization processes that have created our modern, industrialized world. As far as the plants are concerned, those from Europe came to North America with the earliest white settlers beginning in the mid-1600s to be used for food, fodder, and medicine. Shortly after their arrival, many of these plants began spreading on their own, following in the footsteps of the Europeans who cut down the native forests as they moved west. Asian plants, for the most part, did not arrive in North America until the 1880s, when trade with Japan and China began expanding. Many of these Asian species were originally introduced for ornamental purposes – as opposed to food and medicine – and began spreading on their own in the 1930s and '40s.

With the help of wind and birds, many of these immigrant plants – together with a number of North American species that found the Spit to their liking – established a cosmopolitan ecology on the site once the landfilling stopped. Regardless of where they originated, the plants that now grow in Tommy Thompson Park are – by definition – tolerant of the conditions created by dumping rubble in the lake. The technical name for this type of vegetation is "ruderal," derived from the Latin word *rudus*, meaning broken stone.

The colonization of Tommy Thompson Park is similar to the process that happened towards the end of World War II after Allied bombing reduced the city of Berlin to rubble. Within a year or so after the war ended, plants started colonizing the piles of debris scattered across the city, and ecologists who lived there – with nowhere else to ply their trade – documented the succession process that ultimately culminated in the development of woodlands. Such was the birth of modern urban ecology. With Tommy Thompson Park, it's not so much a phoenix rising from the ashes of war as it is a concrete island emerging from the waters of Lake Ontario – an urban Krakatoa, if you will.

In an urban context, the traditional dichotomy between native and non-native species has little meaning. In building our cities, people have wiped out most of the native vegetation and replaced it with buildings, roads, and intensively managed landscapes. The supposedly native vegetation of any city today is basically a historical reference to what was growing there before the city was built and has little relevance to the conditions that currently exist. By extension, the definition of an invasive species has little meaning in an urban context because it requires the displacement of native species that were pretty much eliminated during the construction of the city. Like it or not, the cosmopolitan array of plants and animals that inhabit Tommy Thompson Park have become its *de facto* native flora and fauna.

Given that nothing is native to a landfill jutting out into a lake, Tommy Thompson Park is the perfect example of what ecologists refer to as a "novel" ecosystem that has no analogue with any assemblage of organisms found in nature. As such, the park presents a unique opportunity to study the processes whereby the forces of urbanization, globalization, and climate change interact to produce functional ecosystems adapted to rapidly changing environmental conditions. While the ecological future of planet Earth is uncertain – and therefore scary – the existence of Tommy Thompson Park offers a reason for optimism, because it shows that nature is both willing and able to help clean up the mess that people have made of the planet.

Building the Leslie Street Spit

Wayne Reeves

In *Toronto the Wild: Field Notes of an Urban Naturalist,* Wayne Grady describes the Leslie Street Spit as "a human construct composed entirely of rubble from Toronto's wrecking frenzy of the 1970s, when most of the downtown core's venerable buildings were torn down to make room for such architectural innovations as the Eaton Centre and the [Toronto-Dominion Centre]."

Grady correctly ascribes the Spit's foundations as the product of culture, but his historical sketch oversimplifies matters. The Spit has *continuously* been under construction (and subject to the forces of natural succession beloved by Grady and others) since the late 1950s. And while demolition material helped build the Spit, other sources (like subway excavation spoil and main harbour channel dredgeate) may have been more important.

Working chronologically across the landform's individual parts, this essay examines the multiple rationales for building the Spit and the various methods of constructing it. The original builders imagined the place decades before filling began, envisioning a second harbour rather than a park. The purposes of the Spit were reimagined frequently, due to changing port requirements, community activism, and the rise of an ecological ethos.

One constant in the Spit's development is its opportunistic role as a waste repository, housing the by-products of post-war urban development. In its early years, the Spit received material that was poorly understood as being contaminated. Steps were later taken to accept only "clean" material, as environmental regulations improved. Now, the landform is the deliberate destination for polluted sediments accumulated from an entire watershed (Fig. 6).

Bay and Marsh

The story begins not with the Spit per se, but with Toronto's penchant, over 170 years, for filling in and reshaping its waterfront to make productive land. The Spit is literally the outgrowth of the Port Lands, which in turn were once Ashbridges Bay (named after Sarah Ashbridge and her family, who settled beside the marsh in 1793) – over five square kilometres of sand, marsh, and shallow water, one of the largest and most productive coastal wetlands in the Great Lakes system (Fig. 7).

Dreams of converting Ashbridges Bay into something of economic value date back to the 1880s. But these early plans were no match for the ambitions of the Toronto Harbour Commissioners (THC, now PortsToronto). Its 1912 development plan reshaped 14 kilometres of the waterfront between Woodbine Avenue and the Humber River, with Ashbridges Bay as its chief target. Supported by all orders of government, filling of the Bay began in 1914, forming the Port Industrial District by 1930.

In 1972, students of the Toronto Island Public School took stock of Toronto's past, present, and future waterfronts (Fig. 8). The Leslie Street Spit was depicted in its current and proposed state. The students could not know that "CONCEPTUAL 1985"

Fig. 6
Trucked fill builds the Endikement at the Spit, c. 1980-88. (City of Toronto Archives, Series 1465, File 148, Item 2)

Fig. 8

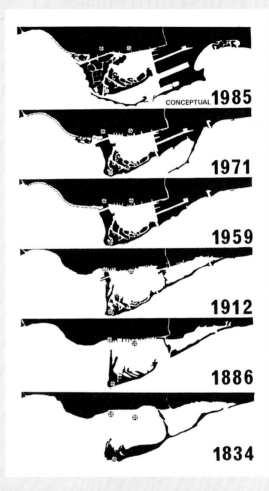

Fig. 7
The marshes and open water of Ashbridges Bay, 1904. This view looks north, possibly from the lakefront sandbar enclosing the wetland. (City of Toronto Archives, Fonds 200, Series 376, File 4, Item 63)

Fig. 8
Toronto's changing shoreline, showing actual conditions from 1834 to 1971 and its proposed state in 1985. (Students of Toronto Island Public School, "A History of the Toronto Islands")

Fig. 9
The Harbour Commission's Outer Harbour plan, 1949. Substantial filling is proposed between the East Gap and Coatsworth Cut; berthage is protected by an offshore breakwater. (*Toronto Daily Star*, March 26, 1949)

Fig. 7

Fig. 9

would never materialize, but they may have been aware that the same institution that had destroyed Ashbridges Bay was now creating the Spit.

Baselands

As the Saint Lawrence Seaway moved towards completion in the 1950s, the THC built new facilities for ocean-going ships. Since the size and cargo-handling requirements of these vessels had rendered the dockwall profile west of Yonge Street obsolete, the THC focused on the East Bayfront and the Port Lands. By 1960, new dockage and three marine terminals were finished, and work had begun on a new Outer Harbour for Toronto.

The idea of a second Toronto harbour dates back to the late 1920s. A proposed breakwater would have allowed the entire shoreline between the East Gap and Coatsworth Cut to be industrialized, but without financial support from Ottawa, the project languished. In 1949, the THC and the City agreed that the idea should be revived, eliminating the park features proposed in 1912 (Fig. 9). A small pocket of fill was placed at the foot of Leslie Street, representing the first work on the Spit (Fig. 10). After a decade of studies, the THC formally adopted a $60-million project for an Outer Harbour in 1960.

Construction had, in fact, begun the previous year on the project, which offered an inexpensive, convenient way of dealing with the development industry's by-products. In 1959, trucks began dumping fill at the foot of Leslie Street, creating land at a rate of seven hectares per year. As one local newspaper observed, "Metro Toronto's building boom is not only spreading joy over the economy, it is also helping to create a brand new harbour for the city."

Source material for the Baselands possibly came from Regent Park South, St. James Town, the Bloor-Danforth subway (Keele to Woodbine), the Yonge-University subway extension (Union to St. George), Toronto's New City Hall, and the Toronto-Dominion Centre. Demolition rubble (bricks, concrete, and asphalt) and excavation materials (subsoil and bedrock) likely predominated, but "non-controlled fill" and "miscellaneous solid waste" meant more than tin cans from the nearby municipal incinerator. A recent archaeological study of the 1964 fill area found household debris, personal items, and even food waste.

Roughly taking the shape of an inverted triangle straddling Leslie Street from north of Unwin Avenue, the Baselands landform was also completed in 1964. The following year, the skinny Outer Harbour East Headland erupted from the Baselands, creating what most people think of as "the Spit."

Headland

The Headland was intended to enclose Toronto's new Outer Harbour, using trucked fill costing 6 per cent of the cost of a conventional concrete breakwater. This "dirt cheap" solution (as the THC put it) took material from development sites within a ten-kilometre radius. The Headland was said to be composed of "clean" fill, but there were other problematic materials.

In 1974, the THC decided to ban the dumping of incinerator residue, battery casings, coal ash, and dredged sediment. Concerns about contaminated soil meant that only rubble was accepted in 1977 and 1978, to the chagrin of the construction industry. The soil moratorium would be lifted in 1979 once a new inspection protocol was implemented, though many trucks still carried toxic material.

By that date, the Headland had almost reached its final length, extending 4.4 kilometres from the Baselands. Receiving up to 1,600 truckloads of fill and growing by 3.5 metres per day, the Headland may have drawn material from four new downtown bank towers, two subway extensions, the Alexandra Park housing complex, the CN Tower, and the Eaton Centre.

Despite the absence of a detailed plan, the THC soon touted the Spit as a "large, well-situated industrial site for future

Fig. 10

Fig. 10

Lakefilling at the foot of Leslie Street (lower left), November 1949. Filling is also underway to expand the site of the future R.L. Hearn Thermal Generating Station west of Leslie. (PortsToronto Archives, PC18/2/2214)

Fig. 10

Lakefilling at the foot of Leslie Street (lower left), November 1949. Filling is also underway to expand the site of the future R.L. Hearn Thermal Generating Station west of Leslie. (PortsToronto Archives, PC18/2/2214)

Fig. 11

The "Central Sector" of Metro Toronto's waterfront plan, 1967. The primarily residential Harbour City meant the relocation of both port and airport functions. The entire Outer Harbour shoreline is proposed for industrial use. (Metropolitan Toronto Planning Board, "The Waterfront Plan for the Metropolitan Toronto Planning Area")

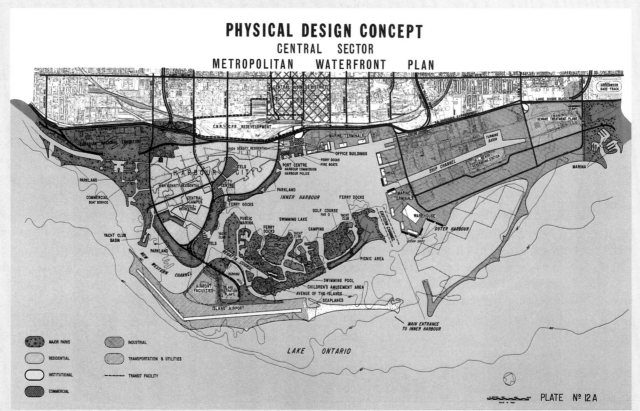

Fig. 11

commercial enterprise." More definition came through the 1967 Metropolitan Toronto Waterfront Plan, soon recast by the THC as "A Bold Concept." Port functions were consolidated on the east side of the harbour; the Headland would enclose a water area two-thirds the size of the Inner Harbour, doubling the port's capacity (Fig. 11).

But the THC's Seaway-related work was being viewed with skepticism as early as 1966. Containerization, rail and truck competition, federal transport policies, and the actions of international shipping conferences prompted a downward spiral in local port activity. Toronto's total and coastwise general cargo tonnages peaked in 1969, while overseas tonnages reached their zenith in 1972.

Efforts to reserve the Spit as a transportation facility ended at that time. In 1969, the THC and the federal Department of Transport had explored the possibility of building Toronto's second major airport on the Headland. Opposition from local residents, led by the pressure group forWARD 9, helped quash the idea. The Island Airport remained in place, while a site in Pickering was earmarked for the major airport. The Spit was left searching for a new function.

Peninsulas and Embayments

Clarity came in 1972 with a pair of announcements by the federal government. Toronto voters were promised parkland as the outcome of a new port strategy for the city. The 76-hectare Aquatic Park would emerge once the East Gap became Toronto's shipping entrance. The redundant port area west of Yonge Street would become the 35-hectare Harbourfront.

Aquatic Park was to arise by dredging the new Main Harbour Channel, the Outer Harbour navigational channel, and widening the East Gap to Seaway depth. As the genesis of today's Tommy Thompson Park, 8.5 million cubic metres of sand and silt from the lake bottom would be placed on the north side of the Headland, creating a set of peninsulas and embayments.

Test dredging occurred in 1972, with the bulk of the $10-million project undertaken in 1973–74. Upon completion, 63 hectares of land were added to the 95 hectares made elsewhere on the Spit since 1959.

As for recreational use, the THC opened the site to organized groups in 1972 and to the public generally on a regular basis in 1973. The site became a popular destination for cycling, walking, and nature study. By 1976, the Toronto Field Naturalists' Club was pointing out the ecological value of "this apparently derelict area." In 1977, the Aquatic Park Sailing Club established moorings in Embayment C.

Formal park planning for the Spit began in 1973, led by Metropolitan Toronto and Region Conservation Authority (MTRCA, now TRCA). The $26-million plan adopted by MTRCA in 1976 included a marina, boat club facilities, campgrounds, parking for 2,000 cars, and ultimately a hotel and amusement facility (Fig. 12). A new planning process tied to an environmental assessment began in 1983, responding to the Spit's emerging ecologies and environmental advocates.

To counter the prospect of a park divided into intensive recreation and managed natural areas, the Friends of the Spit (FOS) issued an "all-natural" plan in 1987. MTRCA's 1989 plan retained substantial car access, but, following additional consultations, an addendum prepared in 1992 largely reflected FOS's vision. The $3.3-million plan approved by the Province in 1995 has been implemented slowly. Trails and a bird research station (2013) were built on the lands made for Aquatic Park; offshore, northern pike spawning channels were cut into Embayments B and C (1997), while Embayment D was enclosed by a berm to create a 5.8-hectare coastal hemi-marsh (2012).

Endikement

MTRCA's master plan referenced another Spit landform – the Endikement – resulting from the Great Lakes Water Quality Agreement (GLWQA), first signed by Canada and the U.S. in

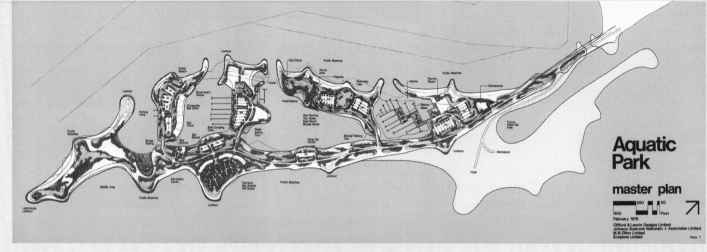

Fig. 12

Fig. 12

MTRCA's first master plan for Aquatic Park, 1976. The intensive approach to recreational facility development would be abandoned in later plans. (Clifford & Lawrie Designs Ltd., "Aquatic Park")

Fig. 13

The THC's Port Industrial Area Concept Plan, 1988. The Baselands west of Leslie Street were divided between marina-related uses and a "business park"; sports fields were proposed to the east. (Toronto Harbour Commissioners, Port and Harbour of Toronto, January 1990)

Fig. 14

MTRCA's proposed landfill program at the Spit, 1988. The Toplands, located east of the Headland tip and south of the arm enclosing Cell 3 of the Endikement, were proposed to be filled in 1990–91, but work continued until 2003. (MRTCA/Walter H. Kehm)

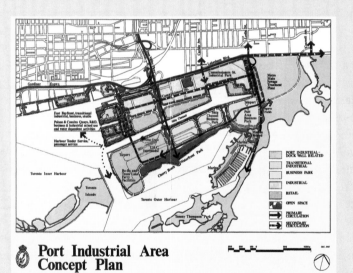

Port Industrial Area Concept Plan

Fig. 13

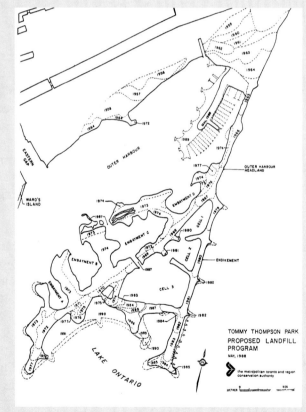

TOMMY THOMPSON PARK
PROPOSED LANDFILL
PROGRAM
MAY, 1988

the metropolitan toronto and region conservation authority

Fig. 14

1972. Previously, contaminated sediments had accumulated in the Keating Channel (the concrete-lined end of the Don River) before being dredged and dumped either in the deep open waters of Lake Ontario or in front of the advancing Headland to be covered by trucked fill.

The GLWQA brought the open-water disposal of sediments in Toronto to an end in 1974. In response, the THC created a small lakefill arm south of the Headland in 1974–75, filling the triangular basin with 10,000 cubic metres of Keating Channel dredgeate. This test facility proved successful both for sediment containment and for habitat creation. Once the basin was drained, capped with clean fill, and re-graded to create conditions for a functional one-hectare marsh (now Triangle Pond, 1999), similar projects followed inside the much-larger Endikement (created in 1979–85 and enclosed at the south end in 1981–87).

The 1.9-kilometre Endikement bears away from the Headland and is at right angles to the net wave energy approach to the landform. It protects the Headland from erosion, but, more importantly, it encloses a three-celled "Confined Disposal Facility" for Keating Channel sediments contaminated by oils and grease, lead, zinc, and polychlorinated biphenyls. Trucked fill for the Endikement – containing lead and PCBs into the mid-1980s – possibly came from the St. Lawrence Neighbourhood, Village by the Grange, Atrium on Bay, and Scotia Plaza projects.

Cell 1 was filled to capacity in 1985, then capped in 2003 to isolate the contaminated sediments. Atop the cap, a 7.7-hectare coastal hemi-marsh was completed in 2007, then the largest wetland gain on the Toronto waterfront. Cell 2 was filled to capacity in 1997; a 9.3-hectare wetland was added in 2016. Cell 3 will take 30 to 40 years to fill with 2.2 million cubic metres of dredgeate – seven times the amount received by Cell 1. The Headland was breached in 1987 to enable barge-loads of sediment to access Cells 2 and 3 more easily through Embayment C.

An estimated 95 per cent of the contaminants flowing through the Don watershed are contained in the Keating Channel's sediments. PortsToronto now removes about 40,000 cubic metres of dredged material annually from the lower Don, keeping the Inner Harbour navigable and preventing the river from backing up and flooding this part of the city. How this activity will be affected by the $1.25-billion Don Mouth Naturalization and Port Lands Flood Protection Project remains to be seen.

Marina

In the mid-1970s, City planners turned their attention to boating arrangements in the Outer Harbour. Alternatives to the location, scale, and scope of small boat accommodation in the Aquatic Park Master Plan were examined, prompted by the evolving ecology of the Spit, the interim establishment of boat clubs along the Outer Harbour's north shore, and the need for additional wet and dry sailing facilities in that area. A 1978 plan included a sprawling public marina and boatyard on the Spit, providing 1,350 mooring berths and drysail facilities for up to 250 craft.

The THC elaborated on these ideas in 1984. It proposed a pair of lakefill arms extending from the neck of the Spit, accompanied by a marine-related industrial area at the foot of Leslie Street. The latter area – the Baselands – had never been developed after filling ended in 1964.

The THC undertook lakefilling for a quite different marina profile in 1988–89, using trucked material – possibly from the Scotia Plaza project – to create a single 9.5-hectare peninsula extending out from the Baselands. This meant filling in part of the Outer Harbour navigational channel dredged to Seaway depth in the early 1970s.

The first phase of the Outer Harbour Marina opened in 1989 with 416 slips. It was expanded in 1992 to 654 slips. The proposed full build-out, using the current landform, is 1,200 slips.

An adjoining 10.5-hectare Outer Harbour Marina Centre on the Baselands has been quietly abandoned.

Baselands Redux

The oldest part of the Spit would be the last to have its purpose determined. The Baselands were not part of the planning processes for Aquatic Park in the 1970s or Tommy Thompson Park in the 1980s and '90s. The THC envisioned an industrial future for this "vacant" property, including it in its 1988 Port Industrial Area Concept Plan (Fig. 13). A draft plan of subdivision filed that year covered 25 hectares, spanning both sides of Unwin Avenue.

In 1992, the north part of the Baselands were transferred to the Toronto Economic Development Corporation (TEDCO) for industrial development. Two years later, the City of Toronto assumed control of the south end for parkland. Recognizing that the site was naturalizing like other areas on the Spit, MTRCA designated the Baselands as an environmentally significant area in 1993. While threats to the area came from TEDCO's proposed "golf academy" (1996) and a Parks Canada Discovery Centre (2005–06), both ideas were rejected.

Greater integration of this "natural regeneration area" with Tommy Thompson Park came with the implementation of the City's Baselands Trails Master Plan in 2017–19 and the construction of a park entrance pavilion and parking area at Unwin Avenue starting in 2019. For the Friends of the Spit, the latter project marked the *de facto* northern limit of Tommy Thompson Park, ending a 30-year battle to include the Baselands as part of the protected Spit.

Synthesis

Since 1959, trucked fill and dredgeate have made about 250 hectares of land at the Leslie Street Spit, projecting 5.2 kilometres into Lake Ontario (Fig. 14). The landform remains an active construction site for habitat creation and enhancement projects, and for armouring to check and repair the erosion caused by storms and high lake levels.

Despite its aura of naturalness, the Spit is a profoundly human place, an urban sink deliberately created from the waste products of development elsewhere in the city and the region. It's an index of changing waste disposal regulations and changing attitudes towards the place of nature in Toronto – a compensatory landscape of sorts, though it can never make up for the loss of Ashbridges Bay. As a place where ambitions have often outstripped achievements and where imagined futures have been revised time and again, the Spit also teaches us the value and limitations of long-range planning.

Aquatic Park

Walter H. Kehm

Suddenly the Leslie Street Spit became "Aquatic Park"!

On reflection it becomes obvious, since the use of the word *park* was a signature of the 1960s and '70s that inferred open space development with manicured lawns, lollipop trees, and amusements for economic return. Aquatic-themed parks such as Marineland in Niagara Falls and Sea World in San Diego and Orlando opened between 1961 and 1973. Walt Disney World in Orlando and Ontario Place in Toronto both opened in 1971 as theme parks that became symbols of progressive park design.

During these periods Toronto was in the throes of great infrastructure planning that was influencing park design. Transportation proposals such as the Spadina and Crosstown Expressways would have destroyed parks. That led to public protest demonstrations. Construction of the Spadina Expressway started in 1963 and with its progression, the potential negative impacts were realized. Neighbourhood protection advocates such as Jane Jacobs and John Sewell organized groups that were devoted to stopping construction. Proposed development around and in the Cedarvale and other ravines had rallying cries of "parks are for people." These transportation plans were defeated, and the Davis government announced the cancellation of the Spadina project in 1971.

Undaunted, the City still aggressively followed its transportation master plan, which proposed widening arterial and local city roads with significant implications for neighbourhoods. People became alarmed once again. While neighbourhood plans were being reviewed, the future of the 1950s-era Gardiner Expressway and its psychological barrier to the waterfront became a major consternation. Greater public access to the Toronto Harbour waterfront was demanded. Renewal of the federally owned and derelict waterfront lands prompted the government to return major harbour frontage to the City. Toronto's media, political life, and its citizens hotly debated the decisions on what were the best and appropriate uses for this valuable land. The same debate continues to this day. A major consensus was the public demand for more parks and recreation lands near the inner city. The Chicago waterfront green space model was considered an excellent example of urban park space design. However, this waterfront model was rejected and preference was given to the extension of the city's dense urban development. The inner city was planned to extend to the Inner Harbour, car-free promenade edges with attractive paving and tree plantings. Interspersed along the waterfront, small parks were proposed as the forefronts to new building development. The waterfront plan became a massive real estate investment.

In this environment the new "Aquatic Park Master Plan" (the Leslie Street Spit) was published by Metropolitan Toronto and Region Conservation Authority (MTRCA, now TRCA) in May 1985 and followed many of the precedents established in its 1976 conceptual master plan. The plan emphasized the "vast area of sheltered water uniquely suitable for a variety of boating uses." The plan also recognized that the Spit had changed significantly since the early 1970s and, through natural succession, had produced "an environmentally significant area with

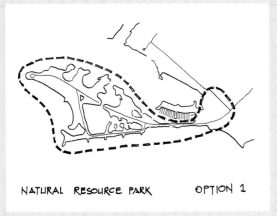

NATURAL RESOURCE PARK   OPTION 1

RECREATION PARK   OPTION 2

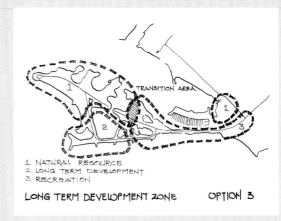

1. NATURAL RESOURCE
2. LONG TERM DEVELOPMENT
3. RECREATION

LONG TERM DEVELOPMENT ZONE   OPTION 3

Fig. 15   Fig. 16   Fig. 17

Fig. 18

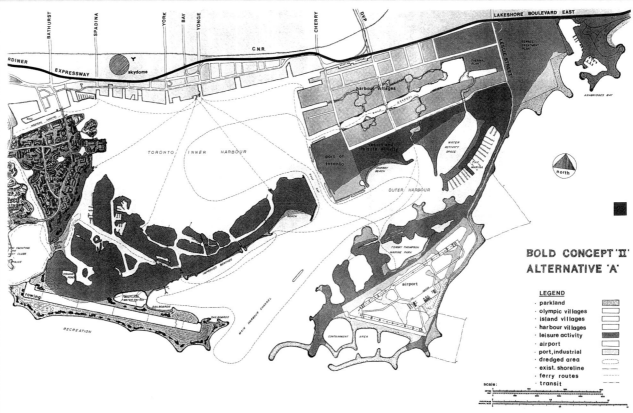

BOLD CONCEPT 'II'
ALTERNATIVE 'A'

LEGEND
· parkland
· olympic villages
· island villages
· harbour villages
· leisure activity
· airport
· port, industrial
· dredged area
· exist. shoreline
· ferry routes
· transit

Fig. 15
Natural Resource Park
(Walter H. Kehm)

Fig 16
Recreation Park
(Walter H. Kehm)

Fig. 17
Long-Term Development Zone (Walter H. Kehm)

Fig. 18
Proposed location of Billy Bishop Airport. (Toronto Harbour Commissioners, Port and Harbour of Toronto, Jack Jones, 1988)

a wealth of flora." Through all those years nature had a plan of its own. Quietly and progressively the barren, debris-littered landscape turned green; plants, birds, fish, mammals, and insects thrived. The little-understood and unplanned aspects were people! They discovered, and continued to inhabit, the Spit for rest and recreation. As the waterfront continued to develop with high-rise buildings, Aquatic Park was becoming the default waterfront green space.

In recognition of this phenomenon a new Aquatic Park planning process was started by MTRCA to guide the planning for the Spit. Three options were proposed:

Option One – A **Natural Resource Park**, characterized as an area with minimal development and to include environmental management, educational research, interpretive programs, and non-development recreational uses including jogging, cycling, walking, bird-watching, canoeing, and fishing. Access for the scow would continue through Embayment C. (See Fig. 15.)

Option Two – A **Recreation Park** containing a range of regional, local, and natural area opportunities with a moderate to high level of public facilities, maintenance, and security. (See Fig. 16.)

Option Three – **A Long-Term Development Zone** that would remain an active construction area with no permanent structures and the completion of landfilling and shoreline armouring in accordance with approved final configurations. No public access would be allowed during the construction period. Tug and scow access through Embayment C for dredgeate disposal would be maintained. (See Fig. 17.)

Through a public participation and policy analysis process it was determined that Option Two was preferred. In its defence the report states, "This option designates the entire site for 'recreation' with the broadest opportunity for maximizing the use of the site for such purposes while facilitating environmental management of the portion of the Aquatic Park designated by the Authority as 'Environmentally Significant Area.'" This position was favoured by a large segment of the public who promoted recreational uses of land and water while having regard for the environment.

At this point the story of Toronto's waterfront and ravine systems becomes fascinating. Critical infrastructure decisions and discussions on the future of the Toronto Islands, Toronto's preeminent waterfront park, were intense. Under the leadership of Tommy Thompson, the Metropolitan Toronto Parks Commissioner, a master plan was developed that would have seen all residential and commercial development removed and replaced with a new park. A new plan was prepared and adopted in the early '60s, emphasizing public recreation. The destruction of the Centre Island homes and commercial structures was initiated shortly after the adoption of the plan. The new park that followed was to be a retreat from the harsh sidewalks and asphalt roads of the city, and it encouraged people to put on their sandals. It offered an invitation, after people left the ferry, to "please walk on the grass!" This slogan became internationally recognized.

The Toronto Islands Centre Island plan included expansive lawns, massive cottonwoods, and willows with nature protection areas along the lagoon edges and some islands. A host of themed facilities were constructed, including the Centreville amusement park; children's farm; mini-golf course; bicycle rentals; maze; rowing, canoeing, and kayaking course; café; change room pavilions; ball diamonds; picnic areas; and extensive bicycle and pedestrian paths. Two of the original residential areas were protected and remain as North America's largest pedestrian-only communities.

After a short ferry ride one arrives at a formal landscape promenade that begins with a large fountain and ends with a fishing pier protruding into the lake. The promenade's origin, with its pleached, rectangular box linden trees, is reminiscent of Parisian parks. Or it could have been a recollection of Olmsted's Central Park Mall, which terminates at the Belvedere Fountain with its background lake. This formal and straight-line axial design intervention was a totally new type of park typology for Toronto. Recreation components were organized around it in a picturesque lawn setting, reflecting Olmsted's Sheep Meadow in Central Park. The Toronto Islands were planned to meet the recreation needs of the rapidly growing city and, with its facilities and neat, mowed lawns, this image was consistent with the City's view of parks and recreation places. I believe many people had a vision for the Spit that would replicate this form of park design.

I recall an interview in the '70s with Ivan Forrest, who was then Toronto Parks and Recreation Commissioner. The meeting with Ivan was to discuss his views on ecology and species diversification through the use of native plants in city parks. His comment to me was that he had completed a citywide survey of the parks and the respondents overwhelmingly stated a preference for grass areas that were neat and tidy with an abundance of recreation facilities that were free of charge.

He dismissed the concept of "naturalization," as it was called at the time, for not being in the public's interests or desires. Neat and orderly summarizes Toronto in the '50s and early '60s, and perhaps more importantly, parks are for people. Naturalization implied a "messy" aesthetic and was unacceptable to the public.

Tommy Thompson's domain as the Metropolitan Commissioner of Parks also included Toronto's extensive ravine system. He ardently defended the ravines from encroachment and said to me that he wanted to keep them as wild as possible. Access points were to be minimal and trails limited to key locations. He felt strongly about maintaining the wilderness feeling of these linear parks and wanted to protect them as the city's "green lungs."

His ecologically sensitive understanding of natural systems and plant succession was in marked contrast to the highly developed lawns and horticultural design approach to Centre Island. This view of protecting wild places in the city is why

Tommy Thompson Park is so appropriately named after him. The Aquatic Park Option Two – Recreation Park plan primarily reflected the "parks are for people" philosophy, notwithstanding the inclusion of the Natural Resource and Long-Term Development Zones. The decisions that followed this designation led to the beginning of advocacy organizations. Foremost among them was, and remains, the Friends of the Spit. Under the leadership of John Carley and its devoted members, they argued decisively to protect the Spit's unique and evolving landscape. The land and water areas deserved to be protected and planned as an ecological sanctuary. The lines of battle were drawn, and to this day the Friends of the Spit continue with their advocacy.

The proposed recreation uses were to serve regional and local users on a year-round basis. They ranged from a formal park to natural areas with aquatic orientation. Facilities were proposed for sailing and sailboards with support structures and access. A sailing study completed at the time indicated a wet berth shortfall of approximately 500 spaces. Other key facilities included an interpretive centre; passive recreation for jogging, cycling, and walking; commercial concessions; sewage treatment plant expansion; sport fishing; and picnic areas.

In time additional uses began to appear that related to the city's parks and recreation needs. The open water cells were to be filled and made into fields for baseball, soccer, and football. There was a shortage of these facilities in the city and the new "free" land provided an ideal opportunity for sports field development.

Other dramatic proposals came forward as the rowing, canoeing, and kayaking clubs felt that the existing Centre Island facility was inadequate. It was not long or wide enough to accommodate competitions. Canada was a world leader in rowing, and Toronto did not have a regatta facility that met international standards. A new 2,000-metre course was designed and presented to the city with a location in Aquatic Park.

The small, inner city Billy Bishop Airport site was also evaluated, and since it occupied a large land area, Aquatic Park was a suggested location. This airport proposal was ultimately defeated, but it was followed by proposals for an Aquatic Park Marineland and aquarium, a historic ship and naval museum, and amusement parks (see Fig. 18).

An Interim Use Program was developed for Aquatic Park. It included the use of a portion of Embayment C by the Aquatic Park Sailing Club, and they were allocated a total of 100 berths through agreement with the Ontario Sailing Association. The park's visitors ranged from 3,230 in 1976 to 22,366 in 1984. MTRCA agreed to operate the park from 9:00 a.m. to 6:00 p.m. on weekends and holidays, provide public transportation, be responsible for site maintenance, and provide a gate attendant, interpreter, and security by the THC functioning as MTRCA's agent.

The Aquatic Park Master Plan had a short life. With increased opposition, led by Friends of the Spit, and an enlightened public, it was decided by MTRCA that another planning process was required to develop an appropriate master plan.

During this extended period, the plants continued to grow, birds nested and thrived, and fish began to inhabit the sheltered waters. Silently and slowly new ecosystems were forming, and people began to notice this marvel of nature. From sterile debris and rubble new life emerged; stories were told and mysteries revealed. An accidental wilderness was evolving from the city's cemetery of rubble.

The Evolution of Advocacy

John Carley

A first-time visitor to the Spit in 2020 would have no inkling of the decades-long struggle to preserve this land as a public urban wilderness. As they walked, ran, or cycled, that visitor would pass through a successional landscape of cottonwood forests, scarified lands, and marshes. On the walking trails by the water, the visitor would enjoy great views out to Lake Ontario and looks back to the city. They would remark on the absence of cars, and on some days, solitude would dominate. The experience would be unique.

Without the advocacy of Friends of the Spit, the waterfront experience we enjoy today at the Leslie Street Spit/Tommy Thompson Park would be far different.

Without Friends' advocacy, there would be a 400-car parking lot and interpretive centre at Cell 1 instead of the marshlands.

Without Friends' advocacy, there would be at least six private sailing clubs and a private boardsailing club, all accessed by car, with a total of 300 parking spaces, all with fenced-off compounds denying access to large expanses of the water's edge.

Without Friends' advocacy, there would be an 18-acre, for-profit golf driving range at the Baselands instead of the wet woods and meadows.

Without Friends' advocacy, there would be three "demonstration" industrial wind turbines on the Spit, impacting the breeding bird colonies and degrading the Important Bird Area (IBA).

Without Friends' advocacy, Parks Canada would have built a 30,000-square-foot building, with a parking lot, at the south end of the isthmus, to promote their parks across Canada.

Without Friends' advocacy, there would be an east-west canal bisecting the Baselands as part of the proposed Lake Ontario Park.

This list could continue with many more private and government agencies' pet projects.

Simply put, without Friends' advocacy and unrelenting pressure, the Spit would have ended up urbanized and privatized, with nature and the wilderness relegated to a decidedly second-place position, in a confined area.

Friends of the Spit was established in 1977 as a non-partisan advocacy group with the goal of promoting car-free access to the peninsula, to allow everyone to enjoy low-impact recreational uses of the land.

That the organization still exists 43 years later is both a testament to the importance of the Spit and the story of how an advocacy group evolved to keep furthering its ideals. Friends of the Spit is an all-volunteer organization, which, at the height of its membership, boasted 1,200 members. As of 2020, mailings go out to approximately 500 addresses.

Into the early '80s, access to the Spit was limited to specific times on weekends. Visitors at other times were deemed to be trespassing, evicted when caught, and threatened with trespassing charges. A late-'70s Beaches Bicycle Club trip out on the Spit was led by a Harbour Police car, with a follow-up vehicle! Years later, a Toronto Harbour Commission executive stated ruefully (to the author) that public access should never have been allowed!

Gaining access for the public, with no admission charges, was Friends of the Spit's first success.

The Spit had been built to create a sheltered body of water ("the Outer Harbour") for an anticipated increase in Great Lakes shipping. Before the Spit was completed, this expected increase had in fact become a decline, and other uses for the Spit were then considered. The prevailing wisdom of the mid-'70s was that the optimal use for this land being created from excavated material and harbour silt would be an Aquatic Park. Colourful renderings of the proposed park illustrated frolicking crowds enjoying sailing and other water sports. While this vision was bandied about, the physical area of the Spit continued to be enlarged and the land became vegetated. The natural succession of the vegetation, coupled with an increasing number of visitors who appreciated that evolution and enjoyed the land as it was, meant that the Aquatic Park plans had opposition.

In opposition to the Aquatic Park plan, Friends of the Spit was soon supported by other naturalist organizations, by cycling organizations, and by numerous citizen and ratepayer groups. Their support lent added strength to every deputation and at every public meeting.

In 1982, the provincial government vested management of the Spit in Metropolitan Toronto and Region Conservation Authority (MTRCA), which became Toronto and Region Conservation Authority (TRCA) after municipal amalgamation. This started a long process of review, of consultation, and then of public rebellion against the master plan proposed by MTRCA staff and consultants.

The concept plan unveiled by MTRCA called for automobile access to an interpretive centre situated well out on the Spit, with a 400-car parking lot, privatization of land for the six sailing clubs' and the boardsailing club's exclusive use, and a natural area that was, at best, only half the Spit.

While this plan was being debated, Friends of the Spit issued their now-legendary "A Better Concept Plan," which used the metrics of MTRCA and their consultants to illustrate that those same metrics could easily justify an all-natural park. Utilizing citizen and public meetings, Friends and allies put pressure on the MTRCA Board with the outcome that, at a crucial vote, the Board dramatically mandated that its staff examine both the development option and the natural park option. This process took a year. Despite Friends' best efforts, the development option prevailed. That should have been the end of Friends of the Spit; the Spit seemed lost.

However, the Aquatic Park Master Plan was delayed, as the environmental assessment portion of the proposal underwent extensive review at the Ministry of Environment. Concurrently, the Royal Commission on the Future of the Toronto Waterfront entered the picture. The Commission held a series of hearings and heard many deputants speak of the Spit's success, its role on the waterfront as a natural refuge for low-impact recreational enjoyment. Friends advanced the concept that the parks along the Toronto waterfront should be viewed as a string of pearls and that each pearl could have its own function: There was no need to cram every activity into every park! Supported by science and numerous naturalist groups, Friends of the Spit advanced a compelling argument for preserving the largest land mass possible, creating unbroken habitat. The Commission (frequently referred to as the Crombie Commission, in honour of its chair) accepted this argument and promoted the Spit as a public urban wilderness. The Commission also pointed out that the North Shore lands were far more practical for day-sailing club uses. The transfer of these North Shore lands from the Toronto Harbour Commission (THC) to the City, which allowed the continuation of the sailing clubs in that location, also relieved the pressure on the Spit from boaters who viewed the Spit as a low-rent, affordable location for their clubs.

With the groundswell of the Commission's support, citizen advocacy, and public opinion, MTRCA went back to the drawing board and produced the Revised Master Plan that governs the park today.

With the premier's appointment of three progressive women environmentalists to the MTRCA Board, the outlook of the Board shifted. In 1993, the Revised Master Plan and the supporting Environmental Assessment were passed. With the exception of one existing 100-berth sailing/yacht club, the all-natural option had won! Although Friends of the Spit had abstained from stating in advance a compromise position, Friends agreed with this compromise, as the Revised Master Plan stipulated that there would be no private vehicle access during park-open hours. This provision would unequivocally mean that the park would remain automobile-free once the park was open seven days a week. Twenty-seven years later, this provision is now being protested by the yacht club members, as the Spit is now nearing the time when it will be open seven days a week.

Concurrent with this process, the City instituted a new zoning plan for the Spit (1986) that acknowledged the Spit's individuality. A zoning category unique to the Spit was created, titled Gr, which mandated only conservation lands, bathing station, and arboretum uses. Marina uses are excluded from Gr zones.

With the Revised Master Plan in place and government funds sparse, the Spit entered a phase where nature took over and flourished, with minimal intervention from authorities. Ecologically, the Spit continued as an outdoor classroom, demonstrating pioneer ecological communities and their succession on man-made raw land. The Spit benefited from the "Let It Be" approach! Aiding the success of the vegetation and the ground-dwelling bird colonies' evolution was, and still is, the "No Dogs" policy mandated with great foresight by MTRCA. To this time, the lands governed by the provisions of the Revised Master Plan were the isthmus, peninsulas, cells, and embayments. The lands at the base of Leslie Street and Unwin Avenue, now known as the Baselands, were zoned I2D2, for medium-hazard industrial uses.

In 1996, three days before possible ratification by the City committee, Friends of the Spit learned of a proposal to develop the Baselands into an 18-acre golf driving range. This proposal was supported by the City-owned Toronto Economic Development Corporation (TEDCO) and some City councillors. A concerted effort by Friends of the Spit with our allies resulted in the economic development committee turning down this proposal. The next year, Council rezoned these lands from the Industrial I2D2 designation to Gr, in recognition that the Baselands deserved the same protection as the Spit. In this manner, the Baselands, although not within the jurisdiction of MTRCA, were protected. Thus, the northern boundary of the Spit became Unwin Avenue.

Having achieved access to the land, having achieved site-specific greenspace zoning, and having expanded and secured the Spit boundaries, Friends of the Spit still had to pay attention to other proposals that would have the effect of whittling away these gains.

At the start of the millennium, the City of Toronto Planning Department began an exercise of planning the Port Lands. Starting with a consultation process titled "Unlocking the Port Lands," many years of community meetings took place. Friends of the Spit became known as an important stakeholder, and Friends' vision of a green connection between the Spit and Baselands through to the mouth of the Don River, with all land south of the Ship Channel declared as parkland, was championed, initially by Friends, then with other citizen and nature groups in support. The vision put forward by Friends entailed that all lands south of the Ship Channel would be zoned to provide a gradient of activity from G and Gm active parkland uses in the west to the passive recreational Gr uses of the Baselands. To this day, Friends advocates this strategy, and, gradually, the City's zoning initiatives are extending the greenspace zoning to include more of the south Port Lands.

Playing a larger civic role, with contacts built up over the years, meant that Friends could envisage the overall waterfront picture. One example was a private cooperative's desire, supported by local councillor Jack Layton, to place three demonstration wind turbines out on the Spit. Leading the charge under the motto of "a green success should not be sacrificed for a green industrial use" and pointing out the damage wind turbines can cause when in close proximity to important bird colonies, Friends caused the three-turbine proposal to be dropped, though it was replaced by a single-turbine proposal on adjacent Sewage Plant lands. Through an Ontario Municipal Board appeal against this single-turbine location, Friends was able to steer the proponent, with the assistance of PortsToronto, to the present CNE location, an alternative site which had long been advocated for a turbine by Citizens Concerned About the Future of the Etobicoke Waterfront.

With the 2001 creation of Waterfront Toronto, a tripartite organization established by the federal, provincial, and city governments and mandated to plan and develop the city waterfront and Port Lands, funds became available for Spit habitat creation projects at the cells and embayments and the construction of small support structures.

The marsh constructions in Cell 1 and Cell 2 have been particularly successful. Both cells were designed to contain toxic dredgeate from the Don River and Keating Channel, and both were to have been hard-capped at grade, as part of a separate environmental assessment. Once the plan for an interpretive centre and parking lot at Cell 1 had been abandoned, TRCA began looking at other options. They developed an underwater capping system, to allow the creation of marsh habitat. This

approach was heartily endorsed by Friends of the Spit, as it brought marsh habitat back to the waterfront. (The Port Lands are the landfilled, former 1,000-acre Ashbridges Bay Marsh.)

With good intentions, Waterfront Toronto commissioned an American firm to design Lake Ontario Park, a "new" park to encompass the existing undeveloped waterfront lands from the Eastern Gap, the North Shore, the Baselands, and the Spit, through to Ashbridges Bay. Unfortunately, the consultants didn't "get" the Spit experience and kept striving for the big design gesture. One big gesture, a proposed canal to bisect the Baselands from east to west, was soundly defeated. The Lake Ontario Park design has never been implemented.

The evolution of Friends of the Spit also meant a transformation from that of opposition to the role of stakeholder, frequently participating in decision-making, working in concert with City and TRCA bureaucracies, to the benefit of the Spit. Nowhere has this become more apparent than with TRCA, where relations moved from adversarial to mutual respect, working towards the common goal of a public urban wilderness.

In its role as a member of the Spit/Tommy Thompson Park User Group, Friends of the Spit advocated for structures with minimal footprint and physical impact. Eventually, after a number of design proposals, the current small entry pavilion, underground environmental shelter, and bird-banding station were realized. Construction of the last building, a small pavilion to mark the park entrance at Leslie Avenue and Unwin Avenue, began in 2019.

With the definition of the overall boundaries secure, the dangers to the urban wilderness of the Spit now relate to various actions contrary to the Revised Master Plan. The private sailing/yacht club's demand for car access when the park is open is one example. On other items, due to not understanding the urban wilderness concept, various bureaucracies continue to attempt to make the park look just like any other city park, to "sanitize" it.

With time, the advocacy of Friends of the Spit has changed to maintaining the Spit as a place that is different from all other parks. Each year, incompatible use proposals are put forward by individuals or groups who think the land is vacant, who clearly don't appreciate the Spit as a vibrant ecosystem. Friends of the Spit membership is city-wide and indeed province-wide, with some international members; Friends could never be accused of "not in my backyard" (NIMBY) attitudes. In the last decade, the model for Friends advocacy could be distilled as "ever vigilant." Gains are ephemeral and can all too easily be changed by political or institutional whim, if Friends are not vigilant.

As a known stakeholder, Friends of the Spit has been able to shape various recent initiatives of trails and access points, including the adjacent Martin Goodman Trail extension, to favour the public urban wilderness vision and maximize Baselands habitat, while, in the case of the Martin Goodman Trail, also benefiting the cycling community.

Through the decades, Friends of the Spit realized that advocacy and stewardship go hand-in-hand, especially in the absence of government presence and action. Members of Friends created the first bird checklist, which was published in 1988. Similarly, Friends commissioned *Plant Communities of the Leslie Street Spit: A Beginner's Guide*, followed by a plant checklist. Friends were fortunate in having many experts in their membership, experts who volunteered their professional skills in both stewardship and advocacy. Friends hosted a number of environment days on the Spit, created self-guided Spit tour brochures, and generally publicized the Spit. From a weekend attendance of 50,000 per year in the '80s, weekend visits now number over 300,000.

It is acknowledged that Friends of the Spit, by their actions and involvement, established the template for citizen participation and for government/stakeholder interactions in Toronto. MTRCA was initially unprepared for continuing citizen involvement. Prior to the Spit, most issues saw a group established and then, after some form of resolution of the issue, that group faded away. Friends of the Spit persisted, and that persistence forced the bureaucracies to establish a means of accommodating citizen involvement. Other organizations, such as Bring Back the Don, benefited from this template and in turn established their own engagement protocols. As part of this process, MTRCA (now TRCA) underwent a sea change in outlook, altering their approach from hard engineering options to more ecologically based planning and construction approaches.

Looking back, what seems so obvious now is actually the culmination of decades of advocacy by the dedicated volunteers of Friends of the Spit and their supporters. The Leslie Street Spit and Baselands have become, as a direct result of this highly effective continuous citizen advocacy, Toronto's most significant waterfront park: a car-free public urban wilderness, open to all for low-impact recreational uses.

Notes

Friends of the Spit has been the recipient of the following awards:

- *Service to the Environment Award*; Ontario Association of Landscape Architects
- W.E. *Saunders Natural History Award*; Federation of Ontario Naturalists (now Ontario Nature)
- *Thank You Green Toronto*; City of Toronto
- *Honour Roll Award*; Toronto and Region Conservation Authority (TRCA)

PORTFOLIO II

previous page

15
The Swing Bridge, Cell 3,
the Endikement and Lake
Ontario, 2019

opposite page

16
Cell 3, 2014

following pages

17
Fishing at Cell 1, 2013

18
The Outer Harbour
from Peninsula D, 2020

19
Triangle Pond, 2020

20
Footpath on
Peninsula D, 2019

opposite page

21
**View of the Toronto skyline
from Embayment B, 2019**

above

22
**View of the Toronto skyline
from Embayment A, 2020**

following pages

23
**Black-Crowned Night
Herons, Peninsula B, 2019**

24
**Cormorant nesting
area, Peninsula A, 2020**

previous pages

25
Aquatic Park Yacht Club,
2019

26
The Sunken Woods, 2020

opposite page

27
Willow tree in floodplain,
Peninsula A, 2020

following page

28
Footbridge in the
Wetlands, 2019

29
The Wetlands, Cell 2, 2020

30
Wooded area in
Peninsula A, 2014

following page

31
The Toronto skyline
from Embayment C, 2020

PART II: PROCESS

Conservation by Design: The 1986 Plan

Walter H. Kehm

"Nature, sentimentalized and considered as the antithesis of cities, is apparently assumed to consist of grass, fresh air and little else, and this ludicrous disrespect results in the devastation of nature even formally and publicly preserved in the form of a pet."

– JANE JACOBS, *THE DEATH AND LIFE OF GREAT AMERICAN CITIES* (1961)

Fig. 19
I prepared this pencil sketch doodle in 1986 based on my first site visit and intuitive perceptions. Natural processes such as wave action, wind directions, vegetative succession, and the potential to transform engineered holding basins into re-created wetlands are illustrated.
(Walter H. Kehm)

Introduction and Starting Points

With the demise of the Aquatic Park plan, Metropolitan Toronto and Region Conservation Authority (MTRCA, now TRCA) decided to undertake a new planning exercise. I began work on the development of a master plan for Tommy Thompson Park in 1985. At that time, I was the senior landscape architect of E.D.A. Collaborative, Inc., and we were awarded the commission after a competitive process. Our practice was grounded in an ecological approach to planning and design of parks and recreation areas. Previously I had completed plans for Bronte Creek Provincial Park, Petticoat Creek Conservation Area, and an environmental analysis for Bluffer's Park, located a few kilometres east of Tommy Thompson Park – all based on natural process and succession principles. It was with great anticipation and a feeling of humbleness that planning and design work began.

A major introduction to the park was from the water. Rowing six mornings a week from the Hanlan Boat Club, I often entered the park's cells and embayments because of the calm water they offered. At times of rest, thousands of Ring-billed Gulls surrounded me. In following years, Cormorants began to arrive, building their nests one on top of the other as if they were condominium owners. On the water's edge beavers were building their homes, oblivious to being watched. Sitting in a rowing shell with the sunrise remains a magical experience: To the west, the towering city with its glass towers glistening; to the east, the silhouette of trees and birds flying gracefully in the morning's light. I was reminded of how vital it is for future park users to have contact with the waters of Lake Ontario and to feel the regenerative powers of nature.

Thoughts on Design

Walking through the Spit today remains a voyage of discovery. One can see different plant communities developing. The sandy soils with good drainage support large cottonwood trees. The original experience of entering a cottonwood forest with dappled shade lingers in my mind. Low-lying, wet depressions were colonized with red-osier dogwood shrubs, their vibrant red stems illuminated by the late afternoon sun. Silt/clay areas were predominated by grasses and scattered shrub planting. At times it was as if I was experiencing a Scottish moor with endless vistas and broom plants moving in unison to the winds.

Walking through the diversity of habitats, thoughts emerged on the why, where, and how questions that had to be addressed if the master plan was to be successful. How did nature work to regenerate this site? What level of human intervention was required? Where did the seed sources come from? How did the site fit into a regional ecological context? These questions led to the realization that the plan had to address solar exposure, wind directions and velocities, soils, landforms and their topographic grading, and drainage. The plant associations that evolved would be reflective of these site determinants. In addition, the plan had to recognize international bird and fish migration patterns and assess how to accommodate the potentially large variety of species.

As the design process evolved I began to think of these factors as under an umbrella concept of "Conservation by Design." Ecologically based design principles and objectives were developed in association with desired aesthetic qualities. These principles were adopted by MTRCA in the master plan and continue to be implemented.

The diagrams that follow indicate wind directions and the microclimates that can be created with landform topography de-

sign. The design process had to include landform orientation and heights to create hot, dry slopes and wet, cooler aspects. Site grading could vary from gradual to steep slopes, always considering climatic orientation. Drainage related to landform and grading would, by design, create run-off conditions for ephemeral ponding as well as surface flow patterns. The aesthetic attributes would create a subtle flowing of landforms that interplay into a graceful composition.

An inventory of the site's land and water configurations was important to gain an understanding of how and where airborne seeds would arrive and be deposited. Questions arose in my mind about what plant species and their seed characteristics could be expected to colonize the site! Were there nearby airborne seed sources?

What birds would inhabit the Spit and deposit seeds in their guano? Would vegetative debris wash onto the shores and germinate? What water temperatures could be predicted, and would the cells and embayments become refuge areas for fish and amphibians? A knowledge of these variables was important for understanding how conservation by design could be realized.

The planning and design process encompassed a period of two years, with the first year devoted to understanding the site's ecological conditions that would answer these questions. Simultaneously, numerous public round table meetings were held to encourage the involvement of people with diverse backgrounds to share their knowledge and experiences. The three "B" groups of bikers, birders, and boaters clearly expressed their interests. It was thought that there would never be a consensus; however, public discourse over time allowed all parties to reach a new level of understanding and agreement. In retrospect, this was one of the most rewarding aspects of the design process as the appreciation of the Spit's unique, unfettered wild qualities was compelling and of great importance to the city and its inhabitants. Citizen naturalists were of great importance in revealing the site's qualities and complexities.

Policy and Program Recommendations

The policy and program recommendations that evolved are as follows:

- The entire site would be a car-free zone, with the exception of a modest parking lot to be located next to the main entrance gates
- The Aquatic Park Sailing Club would continue to occupy its exiting site with car access and boat number restrictions
- Construction access would be maintained, restricting public access times to the evenings after 4 p.m., weekends, and holidays
- MTRCA and PortsToronto would be jointly responsible for the protection and maintenance of the park
- Significant species would be protected
- Environmentally significant areas would be protected
- Aquatic and terrestrial habitats would be enhanced
- Public recreational opportunities would be provided
- An interpretive centre would be located near Cell 1

Concept Plan Evolution

The approved concept plan evolved after a public review. The consensus plan was based on the following principles:

- Be consistent with the goals and objectives formulated for Tommy Thompson Park
- Be able to protect and significantly expand the natural resource area from the Interpretive Centre to the lighthouse
- Be consistent with the City of Toronto Central Waterfront Plan and Policies
- Be responsive to public input on the alternative concept plans
- Enhance the public's accessibility and opportunity to enjoy Tommy Thompson Park and its unique waterfront opportunities
- Be able to recognize the significance of the Outer Harbour and its unique opportunities for recreational boating and other water-related activities (MTRCA 1989)

Four Natural Resource Zones were identified that were essential for the protection and conservation of the urban wild habitat (Fig. 20). They are:

- Managed succession area – to be designed with a variety of grading and drainage landscapes with different soil types allowing for variety in the natural succession process
- Environmental management area – to be managed for diversity and natural ecological processes
- Preservation area – managed to maintain the presence of environmentally significant plant and animal species
- Protection area – an ecologically significant area to be protected from human disturbance

The Design: Walking, Wandering, and Cycling – Lost in the City

The site had an existing construction road for heavy vehicle access. With its wide scale and central location on the Spit, it was immediately obvious that it would be ideal to serve as the main path for bicycles and people. However, it did not bring people to the water edges and the views they offered. It was important to create narrow, meandering trails where people could wander and immerse themselves in the evolving landscape spaces. Pedestrian-only trails were proposed and developed, bringing people through forests and meadows to the water's edge. In my design experience, people love to discover little nooks and crannies and retreat from the designed, "beaten path." I reflect now on how I see new parks today being overly designed using the latest clichés.

Viewing points were located at key vantage points along the trails to see the dramatic city skyline or gaze to the infinite Lake Ontario vistas. Paths were designed to be narrow and curved to encourage slow walking and be restful as various vistas and landscapes unfolded. From the main Multi-Use Trail that accommodates pedestrians, bikes, emergency and construction and special use vehicles, the narrower meandering hiking paths lead to the water edges or other landscapes

Fig. 20

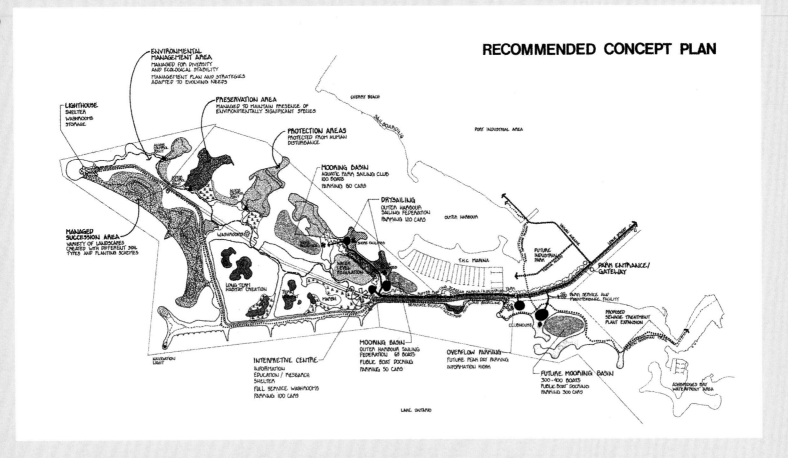

RECOMMENDED CONCEPT PLAN

Fig. 20

This plan represents the synthesis of the outcomes of the public participation process, discussions with the TRCA and other public agencies, and the concept plan prepared by the consultants upon completion of their detailed site analysis, inventories, and evaluation of alternatives. The plan portrays Tommy Thompson Park as an urban wild with proposals for wetlands, fisheries, and habitat creation; a hierarchy of trails and paths for walking, jogging, and bicycling; look-out locations; visitor and education centres; and the location for the Aquatic Park Sailing Club. The capping of the dredgeate cells and their conversion to wetlands remains one of the most significant developments. (Walter H. Kehm, E.D.A. Collaborative Inc., 1994)

with unique qualities. To this day they continue to be spontaneously created. At the water's edge, people sit on piles of rubble or rocks to enjoy the environment. The planned and organic trails that continue to evolve are related to landscape perception experiences where people seek out their desired locations. These genius loci nooks and crannies attract people because they offer the feeling of being in a natural sanctuary. It is here that the stresses of daily life are muted with mental harmony and tranquility restored.

The Water Cells – Hide and Seek

There are three confined disposal water cells with a surface area of 49.6 hectares. Cell 1 is the smallest with an area of 7.7 hectares; Cell 2 is 9.2 hectares, and Cell 3, 32.1 hectares. Their purpose is to serve as Confined Disposal Facilities (CDFs) for the Port of Toronto and the Keating Channel. The cells receive scow-transported dredgeate from these areas and, once filled to their designed capacity, are capped with imported fill material.

The original impression of the cells was their sterile appearance with functional, straight 45-degree slopes enclosing the basins. Thoughts of the destroyed, original 1,000-acre Ashbridges Bay wetlands came to mind as the cells presented an immediate design opportunity for regeneration. In a modest way the lost Ashbridges Bay wetlands could be partially replaced and help to restore the lost Toronto and Great Lakes wetlands while enhancing the "urban wild" perception of the park.

Then I posed the design question: Why not regrade the slopes, change their geometries, and design water depths suitable for aquatic vegetation, fish, and birdlife? New wetlands could arise out of this "Conservation by Design" intervention. I drew a number of sketches (see Figs. 21–23) to show how the slopes, water depths, and alignments could be altered to create new wetlands. MTRCA has completed wetland habitat restoration in Cells 1 and 2 with dramatic biological results. As part of MTRCA active habitat and management efforts, tree stumps

have been added and bottom elevations were varied to create a diversity of microclimatic conditions. Shoreline edges were planted and rapidly vegetated, bringing about refuge and cover for birds and mammals. On the completion of the wetlands regeneration work by MTRCA, plants quickly colonized the cell edges and surrounding tablelands, including dogwoods, willows, eastern cottonwoods, cattails, sedges, arrowheads, bulrushes, pondweeds, wild celery, water-weeds, and water lilies.

Over the years, however, *Phragmites australis*, a reedy and very large member of the grasses family, arrived and successfully populated much of the cell shorelines. TRCA is currently preparing and implementing management plans to control these grasses.

Large numbers of migratory and resident bird populations can be seen year-round. Fish and reptiles have found new habitats. MTRCA's 1994 Wetland Concept Plan reported that "48 fish species have been found utilizing the Tommy Thompson Park area, 28 of which are considered native, and 23 resident species. Twenty-four species have been collected within Cell 1, of which 19 are native, and 17 considered resident" (MTRCA 1994, 12).

The "Conservation by Design" objectives that were established in the master plan were restated in the Wetland Concept Plan (MTRCA 1994, 20, 21, 22):

Objective One – Utilize site grading and conservation by design principles to provide the four basic zones for wetland plants based on Lake Ontario water level fluctuations. (Fig. 24)

Objective Two – Establish a variety of wetland plants and promote the development of successional plant communities utilizing a variety of techniques. (Fig. 25)

Objective Three – Establish structural habitat by providing a diversity of substrate types and conditions. (Figs. 26–27)

Objective Four – Provide specific critical habitat components. (Fig. 28)

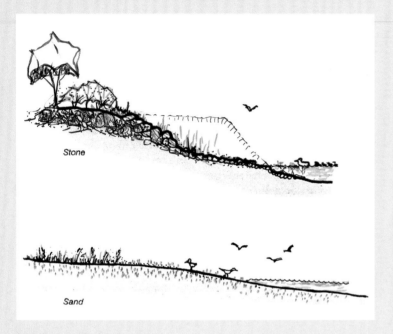

Stone

Sand

Fig. 21

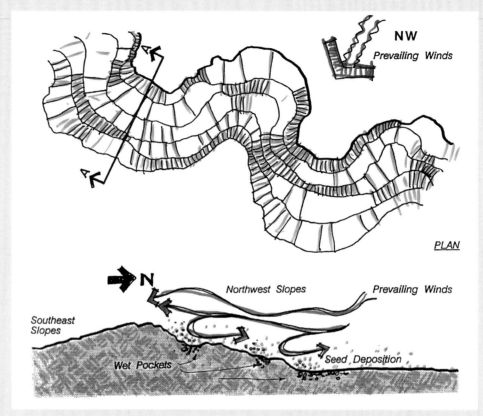

NW
Prevailing Winds

PLAN

N

Northwest Slopes   Prevailing Winds

Southeast
Slopes

Wet Pockets   Seed Deposition

Fig. 22

Fig. 21

Cross sections of the
containment cell reconfigu-
ration for new wetland and
shoreline edge habitat

Fig. 22

Plan and section grading
for drainage enhancement
and wind deflection for
seed dispersal

Fig. 23

Concept plans showing
the original steep, linear
containment cell design in
contrast to the proposed
terrestrial and aquatic
regeneration grading

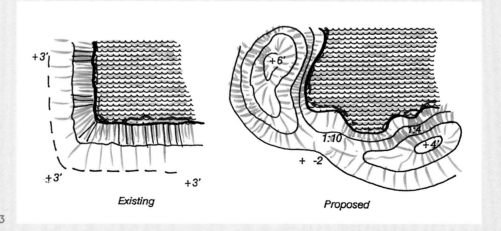

+3'

+3'   +3'

Existing

+6'

1:10

1:4

+4'

+ -2

Proposed

Fig. 23

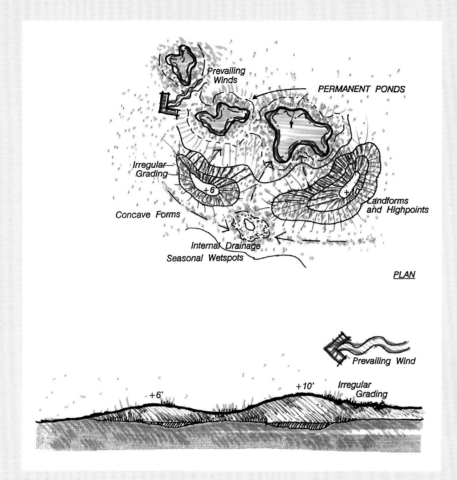

PLAN

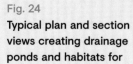

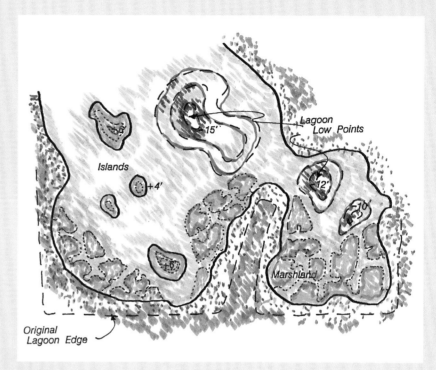

Fig. 25

Fig. 24

Fig. 24
Typical plan and section views creating drainage ponds and habitats for natural regeneration

Fig. 25
Containment cells converted into wetland habitats

Fig. 26

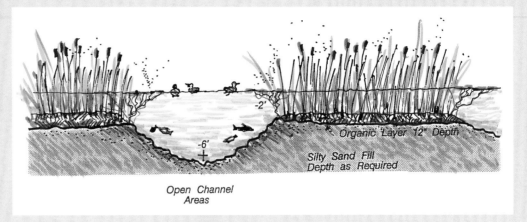

Open Channel Areas

-2'

-6'

Organic Layer 12" Depth

Silty Sand Fill Depth as Required

Fig. 27

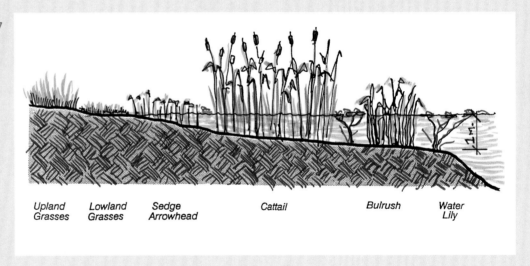

Upland Grasses   *Lowland Grasses*   *Sedge Arrowhead*   *Cattail*   *Bulrush*   *Water Lily*

Fig. 28

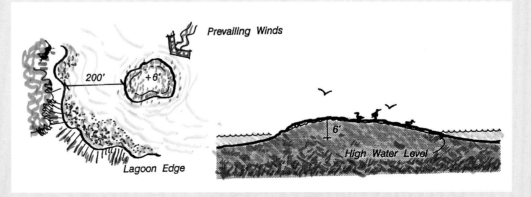

Prevailing Winds

200'   *+ 6'*

6'

High Water Level

Lagoon Edge

Fig. 26

Cross section of wetland edges for fish and bird habitats

Fig. 27

Cross section of wetland edges for aquatic vegetation regeneration

Fig. 28

Wetland cell plan and section for bird island

(Figs. 21–28 by Walter H. Kehm)

In 1994 the site census listed 11 herpetiles, 17 mammals, and 290 bird species.

The Flats and Toplands – Meadows and Moors

This southerly expanse of land was identified as a managed succession area on the master plan. It was conceived as an elevated landscape that could represent dune formations exposed to high winds and hostile conditions. I initiated a design study for MTRCA at the University of Guelph Landscape Research Group to explore how the principles of conservation by design could be developed. The design that evolved created a variety of height and slope conditions related to the prevailing winds and a series of imperfect drainage catchment basins that could decant from one pond to the next. It was anticipated the vegetation that evolved would adapt naturally to the wet and dry conditions created. Today, people have created rambling paths, and with them a sense of mystery, while wandering through untamed moors and wild meadows.

The beach that developed seems like a natural pebble beach that can be found along the shores of Lake Ontario. Wave action has rounded square bricks and concrete blocks into pebble-like sculptural objects that adults and children find endlessly fascinating. They enjoy creatively building ephemeral structures from the rubble.

Distant horizons over the lake are dramatic, offering at times scenes of breathtaking crashing waves due to the high winds. In contrast, there is the stillness and serenity of the quiet mornings. With the rising sun the entire landscape becomes a beautiful and inspirational painting. These aesthetic qualities make the Flats and Toplands unique and create a special sense of place within the park (Figs. 29 and 30).

Triangle Pond – Small Is Beautiful

On my first site visit I was impressed with the expansive new cell areas and the three embayments developed from 1972 un-til 1974, with minor additions in following years. As I rounded the corner of the Lighthouse Point construction road, to my surprise I discovered a small pond with an engineered triangular shape. This interior water body was fascinating, since it was the only pond in the park that could be a warm water refuge for amphibians, fish, mammals, and birds. During the planning process I discovered the pond was to be filled in and levelled! This was a construction intervention contrary to the goals and objectives of the park. As the Tommy Thompson plan developed it was included as a significant habitat area. Over the years the pond has become a distinct microclimatic area with well-developed water and shoreline vegetative communities, a variety of amphibians, a resident beaver house, and significant bird habitats. Unfortunately, *Phragmites* plants have begun to dominate the pond edges and have become a source of concern as other native aquatic species are being replaced.

Lighthouse Point – Land's End

After a five-kilometre voyage through treed areas and water experiences, the land rises. Situated on top is the Eastern Gap lighthouse. People arrive at a "Land's End" terminus to the park, which offers expansive views over the lake and to the dramatic city skyline in the distance. Cyclists dismount and hikers stop to find small spaces amongst the rubble to sit and absorb a truly unique landscape experience. Children play with curiosity and carefree abandon in the rubble-strewn adventure playground. People wander along the water edges and discover unique pieces of rounded clay brick or colourful floor tiles. One can find Toronto's Don Valley bricks, possibly from 1880 Victorian homes; old octagonal white floor tiles, maybe from a Cabbagetown butcher shop floor; and then a shard of pottery from a bakery or kitchen – the urban history of Toronto is there for all to experience and explore. In the wintertime the excitement and drama only increases as the scattered and protruding reinforcing bars from old concrete light poles and concrete slabs become encased with ice and form an embroidered lacework of white crystals. Once again, the rubble, which inspires spontaneous sculpture creations, makes every

Fig. 29

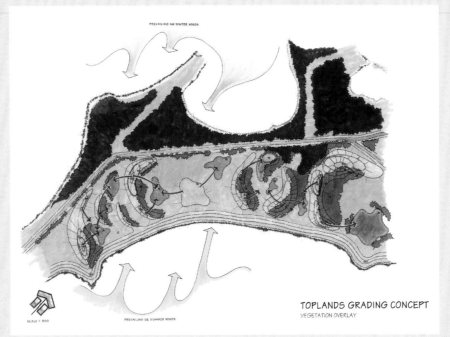

Fig. 29
Toplands plan with grading and anticipated vegetation regeneration zones related to prevailing winds and potential seed dissemination. (Walter H. Kehm and University of Guelph Landscape Research Group)

Fig. 30
Toplands grading and drainage plan proposal to create a variety of landscape environments. They include depressions for wet zones, dry south-facing and cooler north-facing slopes, windy and calm exposures, steep and shallow land forms. These landscape typologies form the soil, water, and exposure conditions that foster a variety of plant and animal habitats to naturally regenerate. (Walter H. Kehm and University of Guelph Landscape Research Group)

Fig. 30

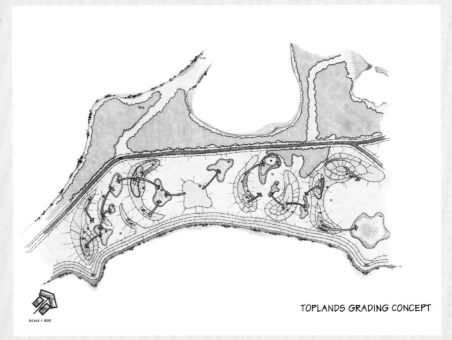

visit unique. It is as if people have a wish to create and add their presence to the landscape.

Embayments and Peninsulas – Voyages of Discovery

The master plan proposed three areas as primary centres of organization for the ecological evolution of the park. Embayment A and its peninsulas had the designations of an environmental management area and preservation area. Embayment B contained the preservation area peninsula on the south side, with a protection area on the north peninsula.

Embayment C was designated as a mooring basis to accommodate 100 sailboats for the Aquatic Park Sailing Club, with limited associated and controlled parking. It was recognized that this embayment had significant ecological value that prohibited any disturbance to its outer peninsular arm and land base.

The environmental management area was designated to allow for diversity and ecological stability. The preservation area's intent was to manage and maintain environmentally significant species. Protection areas were designated as places with minimum human interference and disturbance.

Natural processes over the years have led to significant ecological changes. The Outer Harbour peninsular openings have gradually become enclosed due to sediment deposition, and, with TRCA habitat management projects, the enclosed embayments provide new fish, mammal, amphibian, and bird habitats. The cottonwood trees have reached heights of 15 to 20 metres and, starting in the early 1990s, have become significant nesting sites for thousands of Cormorants, to the point that they are considered a nuisance species. The result of their population increase has led to the death of the cottonwood trees. The regeneration here will be up to Mother Nature.

The embayment and peninsular areas provide many vista points to the city and the Outer Harbour. This has resulted in the development of trail access points by TRCA that terminate with modest overlook areas with rocks for sitting.

The Baselands

This strategic parcel of land is located at the entrance to the park and is bounded on the north by Unwin Avenue, the Tommy Thompson Park Multi-Use Trail to the east, the Outer Harbour access road to the west, and the marina to the south. It was not originally part of the planning process since it was owned by the Toronto Port Authority (TPA, now PortsToronto) and zoned for industrial/commercial uses.

As the planning and design work progressed, it became obvious that this parcel had to be integrated with Tommy Thompson Park. Subsequent negotiations between TRCA, the TPA, the City, and the Province resulted in an agreement to remove the zoning and integrate it with the natural habitat planning for the park. This decision remains of great importance as the land has developed through natural succession with a variety of flora and fauna habitats. It is densely populated with shrubs and trees that provide excellent bird habitat. In addition, a snake hibernaculum and a coyote den are present.

In 2016 a new multi-use trail was developed along the Baselands Unwin Avenue perimeter, linking the Martin Goodman Trail with the Tommy Thompson Park Multi-Use Trail. Throughout the site numerous paths have developed, linking the varied habitats that are especially frequented by birdwatchers (Fig. 31).

Summary – Harmony with Nature and Culture

The Tommy Thompson Park philosophy is predicated on the evolution of diversity and change through natural process with habitat management for fish and birdlife. This is essentially what "Conservation by Design" attempts to accomplish. Through the innovative construction of landforms, perfect and imperfect drainage systems, orientation to prevailing winds and seed sources from bird and mammal droppings, the park's terrestrial and aquatic ecosystems have evolved. As natural succession continues, the park's landscape changes. New mammal populations such as otter and mink have migrated to

EASTERN
CHANNEL

MARTIN GOODMAN TRAIL

PENINSULAS

OUTER HARBOUR

A

LIGHTHOUSE POINT

a

B

b

C

TOPLANDS

GOLDFISH POND

TRIANGULAR POND

D

BIRD RESEARCH STATION
AQUATIC PARK SAILING CLUB

EMBAYMENTS

c

UNWIN AVENUE

LESLIE STREET

BASELANDS

THE FLATS

CELLS

d

VISITORS CENTRE

OUTER HARBOUR MARINA

P

ENTRANCE

3

2

1

ASHBRIDGES SEWAGE
TREATMENT PLANT

EAST COVE

ENDIKEMENT

OUTDOOR CLASSROOM

NATURE CENTRE

ENDIKEMENT TIP

LAKE ONTARIO

LOOKOUT

WASHROOM

PARKING

PRIMARY PEDESTRIAN TRAIL

SECONDARY PEDESTRIAN TRAIL

BICYCLE PATH

MARTIN GOODMAN TRAIL

PALUSTRINE MARSH

LACUSTRINE MARSH

LAKE / ISLAND

SHORELINE / POND

DRY MEADOW

WET MEADOW

BEACH / DUNE

SHINGLE BEACH

L

W

P

SURFACE / SITE
PREPARATION
FOLLOWED BY
NATURAL
SUCCESSION

0m   500   1000

TOMMY THOMPSON PARK PLAN

SITE PLAN
REVISED FEBRUARY 2020

Fig. 31

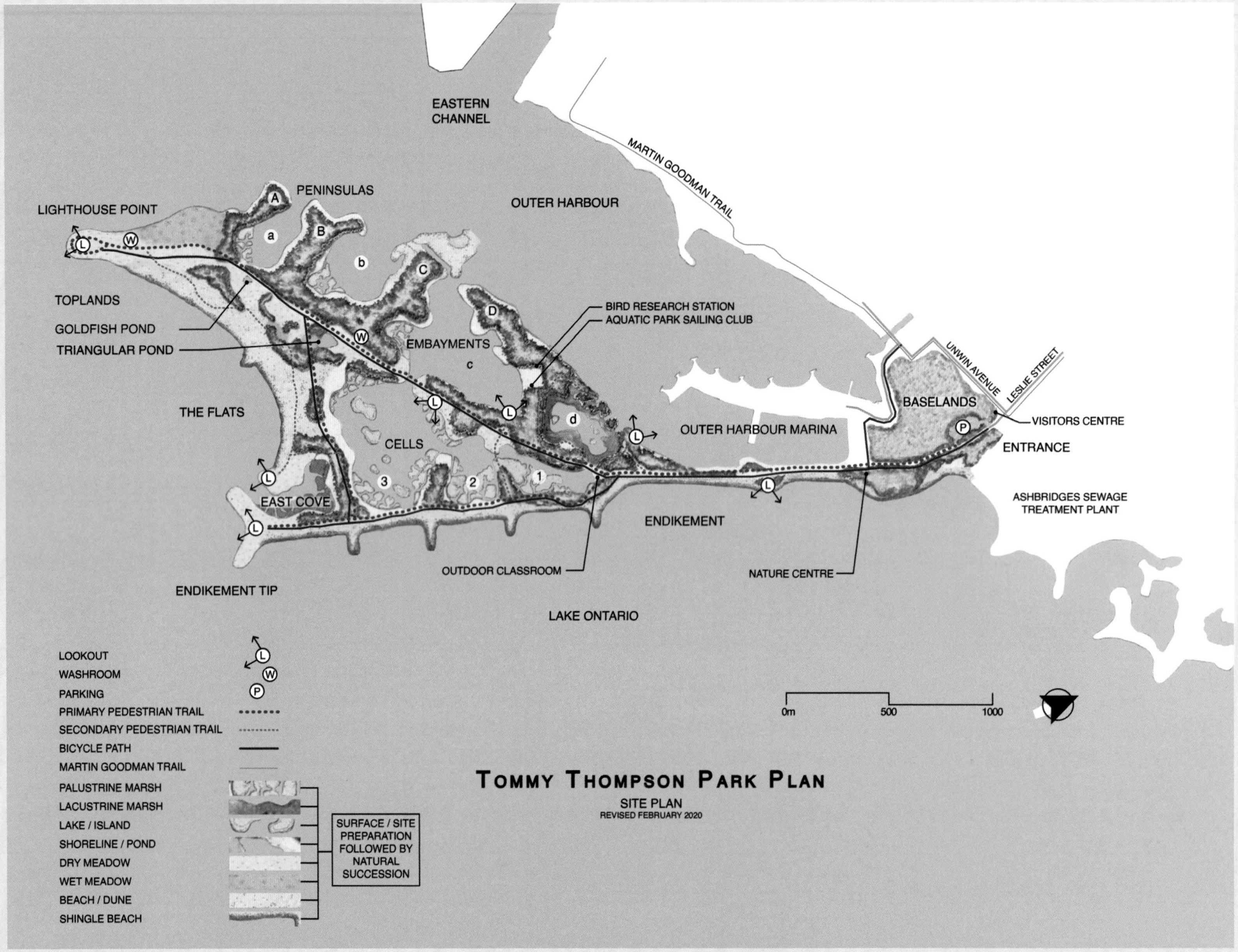

Fig. 31
Tommy Thompson Park
Site Plan, updated February
2020. (Walter H. Kehm)

the park. This has resulted in the elimination of many quaking aspen (*Populus tremuloides*) and cottonwood (*Populus deltoides*). They have been replaced by extensive black locust (*Robinia pseudoacacia*) stands. Non-native tree species such as Virginia red cedar and mulberry are now established in open meadow areas. Birds not often seen in Ontario, such as Canvasback Ducks, Least Bitterns, Black-crowned Night Herons, Great Egrets, Trumpeter Swans, and Orchard Orioles, have become regular visitors. The extensive documentation of the parks flora (see the list of plant species at the end of this book) and fauna provides a rich database for education and research.

From an engineered "spit" an urban wild has evolved into a nature sanctuary offering people a respite from daily routines and stresses. The value of the recreation, creativity, mental health, and spiritual offerings of the park are inestimable. The place of an "urban wild" has been amply demonstrated as a global design model of landscape resilience and diversity.

Plants and Natural Succession

Gavin Miller

Tommy Thompson Park Construction

The story of Tommy Thompson Park's ecosystems begins in the second half of the twentieth century, when it was built as a headland to protect anticipated port facilities. In the early years of its existence, the park became well-known as an example of primary succession: the colonization of new, bare substrate by pioneer vegetation and the subsequent evolution of communities towards a more mature and stable or steady-state condition characterized by higher diversity and more competitive, shade-tolerant species (the current state is shown in the list of plant species at the back of this book). In the past three decades, natural or incidental colonization was augmented by deliberate plantings for habitat restoration.

The Baselands at the foot of Leslie Street were filled in between 1959 and 1963 (Temple 1980). The main spine of the Leslie Spit was constructed between 1964 and 1972 (MTRCA 1982). The growing city provided an ample source of construction material in the form of excavated fill and demolished buildings. In 1973–74, sands and silts from the lakebed of the Outer Harbour were dredged up and formed into a series of peninsulas and embayments on the north side of the main spine. From 1979 to around 2000, a second spine was added to the Spit. This feature extended more to the south and eventually became an endikement enclosing three cells, or large ponds. Two smaller ponds were included on wider parts of the main spine: Goldfish Pond and Triangle Pond.

There are thus two main substrates at Tommy Thompson Park that formed the basis of subsequent plant communities. The first is fill from city excavations. This includes a mix of silty clay subsoils, rubble from demolished buildings, and, in a few places (particularly parts of the Baselands), Ordovician shale that forms Toronto's bedrock (Catling et al. 1977; Eyles 2004). The fill is very compacted, with areas of poor drainage alternating with dry, exposed surface. The second substrate type is the lakebed material deposited on the peninsulas along the north side of the Spit. This is much sandier and less disturbed than the fill and is of lower elevation. It is hydrologically connected to Lake Ontario, with the lower parts inundated during times of high water.

Colonization of Sandy Lakebed Deposits

Colonization of Tommy Thompson Park by vegetation was extremely rapid, especially on the looser, sandy soils of the peninsulas. In 1976, approximately 155 species of vascular plants were recorded throughout the Park (Catling et al. 1977; see "List of Plant Species"). (Counts of species may vary slightly between the original literature and the list included in this book because of changes in taxonomy and uncertainty in identification of a few species.) By 1978, the number had risen to 285 species (Temple 1980). Flora species richness then levelled off, with a slight decline to 226 species in 1982 (MTRCA 1982). The newly exposed sand was taken over by a mix of Great Lakes shoreline plants and ruderal species. Examples of the former included sea-rocket (*Cakile edentula*) and Great Lakes cinquefoil (*Potentilla supina* ssp. *paradoxa*). Ruderal species included horseweed (*Erigeron canadensis*), wall rocket (*Diplotaxis muralis*), and winged pigweed (*Cycloloma atriplicifolia*; MTRCA 1982). The winged pigweed was particularly abundant in the 1970s.

Areas along the immediate shoreline of the sandy peninsulas were sheltered beaches or mudflats. In late summer when the lake level was lower, umbrella-sedges (*Cyperus* spp), toad rush (*Juncus bufonius*), pale smartweed (*Persicaria lapathifolia*), and golden dock (*Rumex fueginus*) appeared.

These early species have seeds that are readily dispersed by water (e.g., sea-rocket) or wind (e.g., winged pigweed).

Concurrent with the largely annual pioneer species, wind-dispersed seeds of cottonwood (*Populus deltoides*) and willows (*Salix* spp), especially sandbar willow (*S. interior*), arrived. These species grew extremely rapidly and remain the two most abundant woody plants at Tommy Thompson Park today. Already by 1976, a few cottonwood saplings had attained a height of six metres (Catling et al. 1977). By 1982, a few trees had attained a height of around 11 to 13 metres, and one had a diameter at breast height (dbh) of 20 centimetres (MTRCA 1982). A substantial portion of the sandy peninsulas was already classified as young forest or scrub within ten years of construction. By 1982, open sand barren areas had shrunk, being restricted to the coarsest, driest sands on the highest parts of the peninsulas. It was noted that this rate of succession was unusually rapid compared to similar scenarios in eastern North America. The exception was nesting areas of colonial water birds, which at that time were largely gulls and terns. The nesting areas remained largely barren but overloaded with nutrients from guano and tended to grow over with annual barnyard weeds, such as lamb's quarters (*Chenopodium album*), after nesting season.

Colonization of Fill Areas

The fill areas were less favourable to rapid growth, due to the compacted soils, abundant rubble, and irregular drainage conditions (some areas extremely dry, others periodically saturat-

ed). In the 1976–82 period, these areas were largely meadow, dominated by white sweet clover (*Melilotus albus*) and squirrel-tail barley (*Hordeum jubatum*), with other typical roadside plants such as Queen Anne's lace (*Daucus carota*), catnip (*Nepeta cataria*), field bindweed (*Convolvulus arvensis*), creeping thistle (*Cirsium arvense*), and burdock (*Arctium minus*; Temple 1980; MTRCA 1982). Native meadow wildflowers were present, though not dominant; they included goldenrod (*Solidago altissima* and/or *S. canadensis*), New England aster (*Symphyotrichum novae-angliae*), panicled aster (*S. lanceolatum*), and heath aster (*S. ericoides*). The meadow fill areas, especially those filled earlier, had scattered small trees by the early 1980s (MTRCA 1982). Along with cottonwood and willow, there were Manitoba maple (*Acer negundo*), black locust (*Robinia pseudoacacia*), Siberian elm (*Ulmus pumila*), tree-of-heaven (*Ailanthus altissima*), and staghorn sumach (*Rhus typhina*). The latter are all typical species of urban vacant lots and, aside from the sumach, exotic and somewhat invasive.

An interesting subset of plants associated with the fill areas were garden escapees that probably hitchhiked as seeds or root pieces (Temple 1980; MTRCA 1982). Many of these would have been brought to the Spit in smaller deposits of fill from yards and gardens by members of the public, who could purchase a token giving them permission to dump their own material. There were both ornamental bedding plants and garden vegetables. Some examples included hollyhock (*Alcea rosea*), petunia (*Petunia* × *atkinsiana*), spiderflower (*Tarenaya hassleriana*), portulaca (*Portulaca grandiflora*), blanket-flower (*Gaillardia aristata*), tomato (*Solanum lycopersicum*), cucumber (*Cucumis sativus*), and corn (*Zea mays*). A few of these, such as the blanket-flower, became established long-term members of the park's flora (see list of plant species at the back of this book).

Wetlands

Incipient wetlands probably appeared as early as the 1960s on the Baselands, which were made from fill starting in 1959.

Temple (1980) described these wet depressions on the Baselands close to Unwin Avenue. They are present to this day. Unlike the wetlands on the Spit proper, these are not hydrologically connected to Lake Ontario and function as vernal pools: filled with runoff and snowmelt in the spring, then drying down in the summer. In 1978, these wetlands included rings of cottonwoods and willows, with the basins supporting cattails (*Typha* spp), sedges (*Carex* spp), and bulrushes (*Schoenoplectus acutus, S. tabernaemontani,* and *S. pungens*). Leopard frogs were breeding in them in 1990 (Kalff et al. 1991).

Other wetlands formed on shorelines and lower-lying areas of the sandy peninsulas. These began as beaches and mudflats that rapidly became colonized by umbrella-sedges (*Cyperus odoratus, C. engelmanii, C. bipartitus, C. fuscus*), slender gerardia (*Agalinus tenuifolia*), silverweed (*Potentilla anserina*), yellow cress (*Rorippa palustris*), pale smartweed (*Persicaria lapathifolia*), European water-horehound (*Lycopus europaeus*), mints (*Mentha canadensis, M. × gentilis,* and *M. × verticillata*), and rice cut-grass (*Leersia oryzoides*; Temple 1980). By 1982, these shoreline shallow and meadow marshes were being colonized by tall, herbaceous species such as purple loosestrife (*Lythrum salicaria*) and hairy willow-herb (*Epilobium hirsutum*). Sandbar willow was also strongly evident at that point, being about one metre tall and starting to outcompete the original wetland flora (MTRCA 1982). Thus, by the early 1980s, the shoreline wetland fringe was converting to willow thicket swamp with patches of tall, emergent forb marsh.

A third type of wetland emerged on a preliminary deposit of dredgeate from the Keating Channel that was dumped into Triangle Pond in the late 1970s. The substrate was heavy silt with a high contaminant load. It was colonized by smartweeds (*Persicaria* spp), with a high proportion of odd garden escapees such as tomato (Temple 1980). This site had the only known record of dwarf nettle (*Urtica urens*) in TRCA jurisdiction. By 1982, the dredgeate area was mostly colonized by purple loosestrife and climbing nightshade (*Solanum dulcamara*). Triangle Pond was subsequently selected for reme-diation and restoration planting, which replaced this weedy community on contaminated substrate.

Summary of Early 1980s Communities

The bare substrate of the newly constructed areas of Tommy Thompson Park, which started as two types (urban fill and sandy lakebed deposits), rapidly differentiated into several broad vegetation communities based on the moisture regime and exposure to Lake Ontario, as well as the original substrate. By the early 1980s, the result was 11 different vegetation communities described by MTRCA (1982), ranging from sand barren to young forest (see Table 1).

Recent Changes in Vegetation Communities

After the initial interest in the establishment of new vegetation at Tommy Thompson Park in the 1975–82 period, systematic flora surveys ceased for almost 20 years, although there are numerous incidental records of individual flora species between 1983 and 1999, often in conjunction with other work. Some of these incidental records were included in the cumulative plant species list provided by Friends of the Spit (1990), and others were provided by TRCA staff. An inventory of the Port Lands in 1990 included the Baselands, and these records were added to the total (Kalff et al. 1991).

When surveys resumed in the fall of 2000, several changes both on the ground and in the survey methodology make direct comparisons with the earlier vegetation difficult. First, there was continued filling and expansion of the land base. This included the addition of new land (known as the Toplands) near the end of the Spit and filling three cells between the main spine and the Endikement with dredgeate from the Keating Channel. Active ecological restoration also began in the mid-1990s. The deliberate plantings marked a departure from the hitherto strict pattern of natural colonization of the bare ground. Second, the methods of survey became

Table 1
**Description of 1982
vegetation communities**

Table 2
**Vegetation communities at
Tommy Thompson Park in
2005–06 and 2017**

Fig. 32
**Flora species richness at
Tommy Thompson Park
(1976–2017) categorized
by Local Conservation Rank
(L-rank): L1–L3 of regional
concern; L4 intermediate
or urban concern; L5 not
of concern; L+ exotic.**

Table 1

Community type	Description
Moist sand beach	Recently exposed sands, largely on the peninsulas. Great Lakes and mudflat species. Transitioning into wet meadows and thicket swamps.
Rubble beach	Fill shorelines (bricks, building debris), very sparse vegetation.
Dry sand/gravel barren	Recently exposed sands on uplands of peninsulas; bird colonies. Sparsely vegetated.
Moist field	Largely on fill areas of the spine; moist and dry field almost indistinguishable. Typical roadside and old-field species such as sweet clover.
Dry field	Largely on fill areas of the spine; moist and dry field almost indistinguishable. Typical roadside and old-field species such as sweet clover.
Rubble beach	Young growth generally under six metres tall with very open canopy.
Pure willow scrub	Mostly sandbar willow; category includes what is likely thicket swamp as well as upland thickets.
Mixed scrub	Blend of young cottonwood and willows. N.B. "Mixed" here refers to a blend of deciduous species, not a blend of deciduous and coniferous species.
Immature cottonwood forest	Blend of cottonwood and taller willow species.
Wet meadow and wetland	Largely meadow marsh at the time with incipient thicket swamp formation. Sedges, forbs, and young willows.

Table 2

Community	2005–06 survey		2017 survey		Change in area (ha)
	Area (ha)	% of total	Area (ha)	% of total	
Beach and dune	22.1	11	16.0	8	-6.0
Barren and prairie	2.5	1	5.1	2	2.6
Meadow	77.7	40	50.5	24	-27.2
Semi-wooded	32.0	17	68.6	33	36.6
Forest	16.1	8	3.8	2	-12.3
Plantation	3.8	2	5.2	2	1.4
Swamp: Treed	13.7	7	22.9	11	9.1
Swamp: Shrub	5.2	3	8.6	4	3.4
Meadow marsh	2.3	1	2.6	1	0.2
Shallow marsh	2.8	1	6.9	3	4.1
Aquatic: Vegetated	10.9	6	10.1	5	-0.8
Aquatic: Unvegetated	4.3	2	7.6	4	3.3
Total*	193.3	100	207.8	100	14.5

* Total area of natural habitat surveyed was slightly higher in 2017 because of factors such as variation in study area boundary, additional filling, expansion of the Ashbridges Bay Sewage Treatment Plant, and differences in lake levels. Numbers may also not add perfectly due to rounding.

Fig. 32

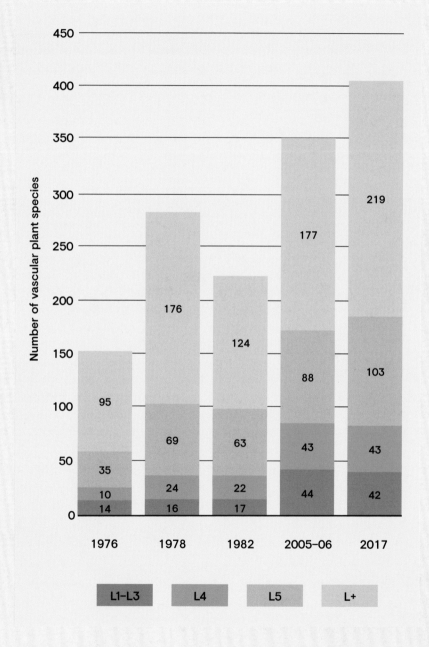

standardized according to the Ecological Land Classification (ELC) for Southern Ontario (Lee et al. 1998). This involves a more systematic categorization of vegetation communities. TRCA began using a rudimentary form of the ELC in the fall of 2000, when Tommy Thompson Park underwent a quick survey. In subsequent years, TRCA adapted the ELC for its purposes. Full ELC surveys were done of Tommy Thompson Park together with flora inventories in 2005–06 and again in 2017. These also provided the first complete plant lists since 1982. Third, digital technology and GIS mapping were rolled out around the turn of the millennium, and the surveys in 2005–06 and 2017 yielded accurate estimates by area of various vegetation communities (see Table 2). (For a more detailed breakdown of individual ELC vegetation types at Tommy Thompson Park, please refer to Table 1.)

The rate of vegetation change has slowed since the 1980s, as the heavier fill dumped along the original spine, the Endikement on the south side of the Spit, and the Toplands area is less rapidly colonized by woody plants.

One surprising change is that forest cover seems to have greatly declined between 2006 and 2017: from 16 hectares to 4 hectares. This is a reversal of the earlier successional process. There was likely some actual loss of forest due to expansion of the colonial waterbird colonies on the sandy peninsulas on the north side of the Spit. Double-crested Cormorants (*Phalacrocorax auritus*) began nesting at Tommy Thompson Park in 1990, and the colonies have expanded rapidly (TRCA 2017a). They are now on three of the four sandy peninsulas. They often nest in trees, though they will nest on the ground. Their guano is acidic and causes trees to decline and die. The cormorant colony areas are best classified as Barren or sometimes Exotic Forb Meadow (i.e., a meadow dominated by non-native, broad-leaved herbaceous plants such as lamb's quarters or stinging nettle [*Urtica dioica* ssp. *dioica*]). Barren expanded from 2.5 hectares to 5.1 hectares between 2005–06 and 2017.

Record high lake levels in 2017 brought water into low-lying areas, and some of the forest observed in 2005–06 would have been classified as treed swamp in 2017; there is an increase in treed swamp from 14 hectares to 22 hectares.

However, it is also likely that some treed areas classified as Fresh-Moist Cottonwood Coastal Deciduous Forest in 2006 would have been reclassified as Fresh-Moist Cottonwood Tall Treed Woodland (a semi-wooded community) in 2017. The community in question would have remained the same: a cottonwood canopy with about 60 per cent closure or slightly less, and a ground layer that includes grasses and goldenrods. The reclassification of some of the forest during the 2017 mapping was due to the persistence of light-loving meadow species under the discontinuous cottonwood canopy. Overall, if one counts the semi-wooded areas, tree and shrub cover slowly continues to expand at Tommy Thompson Park. Upland communities with some sort of woody cover (i.e., forest, woodland, shrub thicket) expanded from 48 hectares in 2005–06 to 72 hectares in 2017. Some areas have been planted with saplings since the late 1990s and had grown enough to be classified as plantation; this covered four hectares in 2005–06 and five hectares in 2017. Open meadow has decreased from 78 hectares to 51 hectares.

Beach communities declined from 22 hectares to 16 hectares between 2006 and 2017. This can probably be attributed to the high lake levels in 2017; much of the area classified as beach in 2006 was underwater for most of the summer of 2017.

Wetland and vegetated aquatic communities increased in total coverage from 24 hectares to 41 hectares. However, there were noticeable shifts in the types of wetlands. Treed swamp areas were not observed in the early 1980s but became prominent by the 2000s. Some of these would have been considered young cottonwood or willow scrub in the 1980s but were revealed to have a wetland moisture regime and ground flora when examined under ELC methodology. These communities included two kinds of Birch-Poplar Swamp, Willow Mineral Deciduous Swamp, and European Alder Mineral Deciduous Swamp. Along with cottonwood, canopy trees include European birch (*Betula pendula*), paper birch (*Betula papyrifera*), and European alder (*Alnus glutinosa*), with some crack willow (*Salix × fragilis*). The ground layer was strikingly distinct with a dense cover of common and Nelson's scouring rush (*Equisetum hyemale* and *E. × nelsonii*). Nelson's scouring rush was first recorded in 2000. The treed swamp communities also had a high concentration of sensitive species characteristic of high-quality habitats, including pink pyrola (*Pyrola asarifolia*) and several species of orchid. Treed swamps occur mostly at the base of the sandy peninsulas of the Spit (with smaller examples associated with the vernal pool wetlands in the Baselands). Treed swamps attained a cover of 14 hectares in 2005–06 and 23 hectares in 2017 (Table 2). Relatively high values for treed swamp in 2017 may have been related to elevated Lake Ontario water levels, which would have saturated some areas that are normally forest. Indeed, the soil surface of some of the treed swamp was underwater during the 2017 survey.

Shallow marsh expanded considerably from 2.8 hectares to 6.9 hectares. This was due to extensive habitat restoration work. There have been many restoration projects; the largest ones are as follows. Restoration work began in the 1990s with the capping and replanting of Triangle Pond (Dupuis-Désormeaux et al. 2018). Similar work in the endikement cells occurred between 2003 and 2006 (Cell 1) and 2015 and 2017 (Cell 2). The easternmost lagoon on the north side of the Spit (Embayment D) was sealed off from the main lake between 2012 and 2014 by means of a fish gate excluding large carp (*Cyprinus carpio*). Exclusion of carp allowed marsh and aquatic vegetation to recover. Unfortunately, the vast majority of the new marsh is dominated by the invasive common reed (*Phragmites australis* ssp. *australis*). The Common Reed Mineral Shallow Marsh community comprised 6.6 of the 6.9 hectares of shallow marsh at Tommy Thompson Park (Table 1). In 2006, this community occupied 1.2 hectares, so it has undergone almost a sixfold increase in 11 years. Given the rapid expansion and to protect the native emergent aquatic vegetation planted in the newly created Cell 2 wetland, TRCA initiated a *Phragmites australis* management strategy in 2018.

It involves treating common reed with a foliar herbicide application during autumn senescence, at which time nutrients are transported to the root for winter storage. The first year of management was highly successful, with a 74 per cent reduction in live common reed within the Cell 1 and Cell 2 wetlands in summer 2019.

Meadow marsh (herbaceous wetlands that dry up seasonally) also expanded slightly. There are a few small, constructed vernal-pool type wetlands on the Toplands, similar to the spontaneous ones in the Baselands. Like the shallow marshes, meadow marshes at Tommy Thompson Park are now dominated by common reed.

Aquatic vegetation communities do not seem to have changed much at first glance. A few species of aquatic plant, such as Richardson's pondweed (*Potamogeton richardsonii*), were washed ashore and noted in the 1970s and 1980s (see the list of plant species), but the communities were not described. In 2005–06 and 2017, vegetated aquatic communities remained steady in coverage, with just over ten hectares observed in each survey. However, the density and diversity of aquatic vegetation increased, especially when Embayment D was protected from carp. This was reflected in an increase in white water lily (*Nymphaea odorata* ssp. *tuberosa*) populations, which had originally been planted. Water Lily Mixed Shallow Aquatic community increased from 0.5 to 5.5 hectares at the expense of sparsely vegetated communities that had only submersed vegetation.

Floristic Richness

Now that the overall pattern of vegetation colonization, community formation, and composition has been examined, it is worthwhile to take a closer look at the total flora and particular subsets of it.

The general pattern over the past 40 years has been an upward trend in plant species richness (Fig. 32). Accounting for the years in which full flora inventories took place at Tommy Thompson Park, the total number of plant species was roughly 155 in 1976. It increased to 285 in 1978, and then declined to 226 in 1982, possibly due to variation in survey intensity. In 2005–06, there were 352 plant species recorded. Finally, the most recent survey in 2017 yielded 407 species. The cumulative total (i.e., every plant that has ever been observed, whether or not it is still present) is 581 species (see the list of plant species).

The increase in floristic richness results from dispersal and colonization of the originally bare substrate at Tommy Thompson Park, followed by increasing complexity and interrelationships within the vegetation communities as they matured. Dispersal was initially by both natural and human means. Natural means included movement by wind, water, and birds. Human means included adhesion to vehicles and equipment or transport of propagules such as root pieces in fill material (Catling et al. 1977; MTRCA 1982).

After 1990, deliberate introduction of new species through plantings became a significant factor. There were 25 species identified as introduced through planting in 2005–06, and 53 in 2017. A few of these were random introductions by park users, such as the prickly-pear cactus (*Opuntia cespitosa*) observed in a sand barren in the late 1980s/early 1990s. Most of them are native species used in restoration plantings, such as tuberous white water lily, Indian grass (*Sorghastrum nutans*), and red oak (*Quercus rubra*). All of the conifers at Tommy Thompson Park, with the exception of common juniper (*Juniperus communis*) and possibly Scots pine (*Pinus sylvestris*), are planted (see the list of plant species).

Conservation Status of Flora

The earlier studies of Tommy Thompson Park noted that a number of rare plants had appeared among the colonizing species (MTRCA 1982). Examples included Great Lakes cinquefoil, sea-rocket, and a couple of umbrella-sedges. Since then, Toronto and Region Conservation Authority (TRCA) re-vised the way that flora and fauna are evaluated for conservation concern. Instead of relying only on rarity, species are assessed according to a set of criteria that includes sensitivity as well as abundance (TRCA 2017b). Each species is assigned a local rank (L-rank) that ranges from L1 to L5. Exotic species are assigned a rank of L+. The higher-ranked species are of conservation concern throughout TRCA jurisdiction. Species ranked L4 are of intermediate concern and show some sensitivity in urban habitats. Species ranked L5 are adaptable and secure. Local rankings follow the North American NatureServe rankings that are applied at the provincial or state (S), national (N), and global (G) scales (NatureServe 2019).

Throughout the history of Tommy Thompson Park, exotic species (L+) have formed the majority of the flora, followed by adaptable, common native species (L5) (Fig. 33). This is expected in a new, disturbed habitat surrounded by urban landscape. However, there have been species of regional (L1–L3) and urban (L4) concern since the earliest surveys. Most of these are associated with Great Lakes coastal environments and were also present on the nearby Toronto Islands. Species of regional concern peaked in the 2000s with 44 species, but dropped subsequently to 42 species. The drop is greater when planted species are excluded; there were 34 species of regional concern that had arrived spontaneously in 2005–06, and 24 in 2017. Restoration plantings partially masked an apparent decline in floristic quality.

Orchids and Great Lakes coastal species associated with the swamps and meadow marshes on the sandy peninsulas were particularly affected. The first orchid, tall northern green orchid (*Platanthera aquilonis*), appeared in 1980 (MTRCA 1982). By the early 1990s, two more species had appeared, including showy lady's slipper (*Cypripedium reginae*). Orchid diversity peaked in 2006, with five native species recorded (see the list of plant species). In 2017, only one native orchid species was found and it was on the Baselands: Great Plains ladies' tresses (*Spiranthes magnicamporum*). Several other plants followed a similar pattern, including fringed gentian (*Gentianopsis crinita*) and obedient plant (*Physostegia virginiana*). They were found in 2006 but not in 2017.

Reasons for the decline in species of conservation concern are not known for certain, but likely contributors are 1) high water levels in 2017 that inundated the treed swamp areas and shoreline marshes where many of these plants occurred; 2) expansion of cormorant nesting areas; and 3) the spread of invasive species into many moist habitats, especially common reed. Nutrient deposition from the birds' guano could also suppress sensitive native species and encourage the rapid growth of invasive species. Prodigious nutrient deposition was already noted in gull colonies by MTRCA (1982).

It is also unclear whether the reversal in floristic quality is a short-term dip or a permanent trend. As lake levels drop and invasive species management takes hold, some of these plants may reappear. Management of the cormorant colonies has also been initiated with the goal of restricting their nesting locations to the ground or previously impacted trees using a suite of non-lethal deterrent techniques (TRCA 2017a).

The current vegetation communities at Tommy Thompson Park reflect a combination of natural processes and later restoration efforts brought in to deal with challenges such as improving habitat, capping contaminated sediment, and controlling invasive species. Restoration will continue to effectively address any issues as they arise. Tommy Thompson Park remains an excellent case study of the establishment and continuing evolution of vegetation communities on new substrate within an urban area.

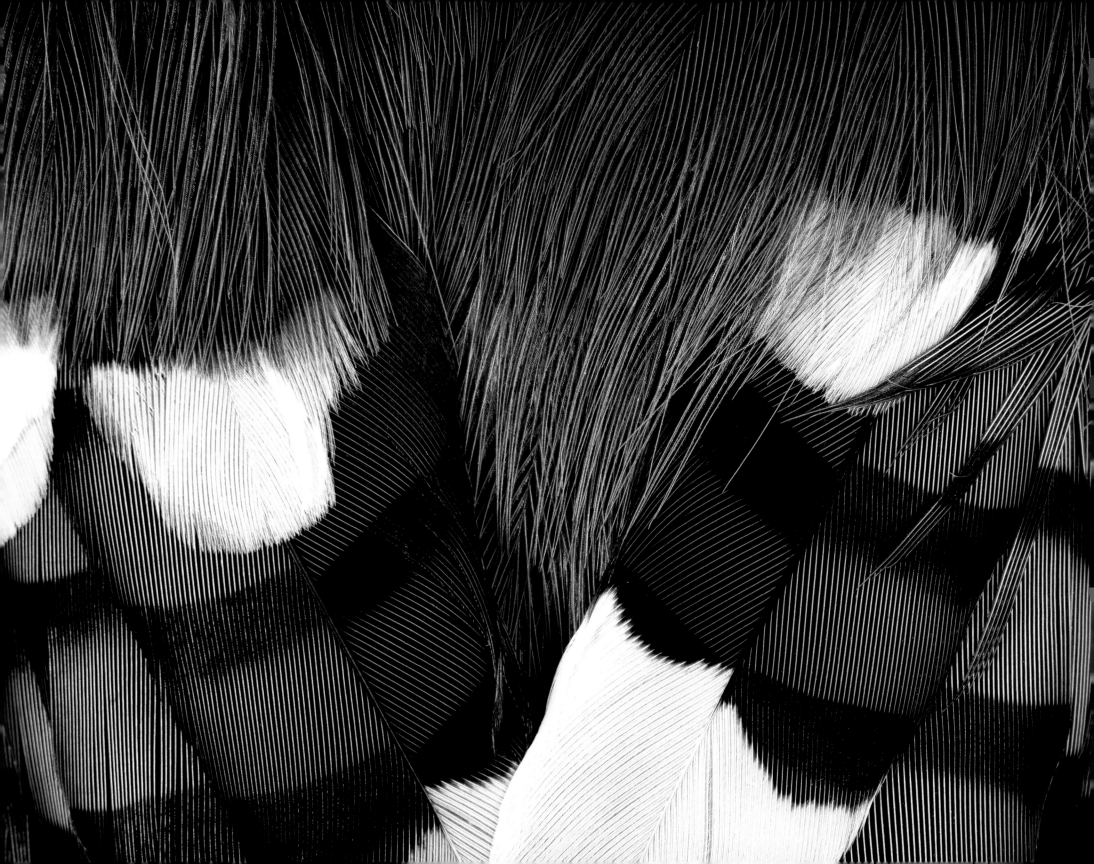

Birds and Birding at the Spit

Garth Vernon Riley

It is impossible to talk about the history of the Leslie Street Spit and Tommy Thompson Park (the Spit) without including a section discussing birds at the Spit and how they helped to define the area as an ecological wonder, unprecedented in a large urban environment.

In the early days, the landfilling operations necessary for the construction of the Spit attracted many people interested in knowing what exactly was taking place. The curiosity-seekers looked over and around construction barriers to observe the earth-moving operations. Among the prying eyes were a group of individuals (birders) interested in seeing birds and who fantasized about the types of bird this newly created peninsula might attract. The birders and other future Spit regulars risked trespassing fines just to see the Spit up close and to see exactly what species of birds it was attracting.

As the Spit grew in size, sections of it were completed and were free of people and construction vehicles. Birds, which are opportunistic, quickly saw this vacant land, free of predators, as a place where they could stop to rest, feed, and eventually nest.

There are two major North American migratory flyways that pass over Southern Ontario and of course the Spit. These flyways are paths that migratory birds have historically taken to travel between their breeding grounds in Canada and their wintering grounds in the southern U.S., Central America, the West Indies, and South America. As a result of the proximity to these flyways, the Spit has become a critical resting place for migratory birds in the spring and fall. Additionally, the sheltered bays and expansive land area provide important wintering areas for waterfowl and birds such as owls.

As of 2019, 325 species of bird have been recorded at the Spit; this is an exceptional number considering that Algonquin Provincial Park has recorded approximately 272 species, and Point Pelee has a checklist of roughly 390 species. The total historic list of bird species recorded in the entire province of Ontario stands at 501 species (based on the results of the 2019 review by the Ontario Bird Records Committee).

Designation of the Spit and Tommy Thompson Park as an Important Bird Area in 2000

As a result of the Spit's significance as a stopover for migrating birds, as a breeding area for colonial water birds, and as an overwintering area for waterfowl, it achieved international recognition as an Important Bird Area (IBA), as designated by BirdLife International (https://www.birdlife.org) in 2000 (Wilson and Cheskey 2001). We must continue to be vigilant to ensure that this legacy and treasury remains for future generations to experience and enjoy.

Seasonality of Birds

Winter (December–February)

The variety of birds that can be seen at the Spit in winter is very different from the other seasons. Large flocks of mixed waterfowl species reside in the inner bays and open waters surrounding the Spit, as well as the inland cells when they are not frozen over. Overwintering waterfowl species include Greater Scaup, Redhead, Long-tailed Duck, Red-breasted Merganser, Common Goldeneye, and Bufflehead. More unusual species such as Harlequin Duck (almost annually), King Eider, Eurasian Wigeon, and Barrow's Goldeneye are possible.

Owls are present during winter but must not be disturbed and should be safely viewed from a distance. Disturbing owls during daylight hours stresses the birds and, since they are predominantly nocturnal, disrupts their sleep and rest. Snowy, Great Horned, Long-eared, and Northern Saw-whet Owl are quite regular but are often difficult to see. Some rarer species of owl that have occurred here over the years include Boreal Owl, Great Gray Owl, and Northern Hawk Owl.

Even an Ivory Gull from the high Arctic made a brief visit to the Spit in February 2010.

Other birds that occasionally call the Spit home during the winter include Northern Shrike, several species of sparrow, Peregrine Falcon, and, in irruption years, Common Redpoll.

Spring (March–May)

During this season the Spit provides essential stopover habitat for neotropical migrants, waterfowl, shorebirds, and raptors where they can rest and refuel for their long journey north to their breeding grounds.

The wonder and spectacle of spring migration cannot be over-emphasized as the migrants are in their colourful breeding plumage and often singing their varied and beautiful songs. One of the best places to view these neotropical migrants is in the "Wet Woods" in the Baselands of the Spit. This area is critically important to these migrants as it is a unique habitat on the Spit. The Baselands are located near the entrance to the Spit just off of Unwin Avenue and immediately south of the parking lot. There is a large stand of mature trees here, standing water, red-osier dogwood, and cattails (now becoming overgrown with *Phragmites*), which provide a diverse habitat. The standing water provides an excellent breeding area for insects upon which migrating birds rely to fuel the remainder of their migration.

Depending on weather conditions, strong south winds can result in overshoots of birds that typically nest south of Ontario. Kentucky Warbler, Yellow-breasted Chat, White-eyed Vireo, Summer Tanager, and Worm-eating Warbler are just a few examples of these overshoots.

Shorebirds migrate long distances, travelling from as far away as southern South America. Like other birds, shorebirds need places to rest and feed along their way to the Canadian Arctic. Species such as Whimbrel, Dunlin, Short-billed Dowitcher, and Ruddy Turnstone are just a few examples of shorebird species that can be found each spring at the Spit. Rarer shorebirds that have previously been recorded at the Spit include Red Knot, Long-billed Dowitcher, Western Sandpiper, Black-necked Stilt, and Piping Plover. Some of the best areas to view shorebirds are in the Cell 1 and 2 wetlands. Another good area is along the rubble-gravel beaches and hardpoints, which provide resting and feeding areas along the lakeshore.

Summer (June–August)

Of equal significance is the number of bird species that have been confirmed as nesting at this location. The number of species that have bred here currently stands at 70 and includes several species that are classified by the Committee on the Status of Endangered Wildlife in Canada (COSEWIC) as "Species at Risk" (https://wildlife-species.canada.ca/species-risk-registry/sar/index/default_e.cfm) in Ontario: Barn Swallow (threatened); Bank Swallow (threatened); and most recently Least Bittern (threatened) (Dupuis-Desormeaux, Sturdee, Johnston, and Xamin 2017).

The first confirmed Canvasback nest in Ontario was located here in 2000 (Coady 2000).

As most species are busy nesting and rearing young during the summer months, the number of bird species to be observed becomes quite low as compared to migration periods. However, the large colonies of water birds are an amazing sight to behold. Thousands of Ring-billed Gulls and Double-crested Cormorants nest on the southern peninsulas, as do smaller numbers of Black-crowned Night-Herons, Great Egrets, Common Terns, and, historically, Caspian Tern and Herring Gull. The sight, sound, and even smells of these species raising young give the observer a strong sense of what a true wilderness area is.

As mentioned, summer at the Spit tends to be fairly slow and low in the variety of species that can be seen; however, rarities can turn up at any time. Fall migration of shorebirds can begin as early as late June and early July and usually involves adult birds that were unsuccessful at breeding. Also, newly fledged birds from other areas of the Americas often wander far from their breeding sites and may turn up here, such as Fork-tailed Flycatcher (from South America) and Tricoloured Heron (from southern North America).

Fall (August–November)

In fall the neotropical migrants that hatched in our boreal forests, along with adult birds, begin their long migration to the south. Similar to spring migrants they need safe places to rest and feed in preparation for their lengthy flights. The fall migrants are much quieter than they were during spring migration as they are no longer interested in breeding. Similarly both the young and the mature birds are in their drab fall plumage, which makes them much stealthier and more difficult for predators to see. Subsequently, they provide a greater

challenge for birders who are trying to find and identify them. Raptors are also on the move and follow the other birds moving south. Their primary objective is to get to warmer wintering grounds, and they often follow the smaller migrants, as they are an important source of food.

The Spit serves as an attractive place for migrating birds in the fall, and it is not surprising that a number of rare species have been spotted here over the years, such as Cave Swallow (from southwestern North America) and Heermann's Gull (from extreme western North America, California).

In addition to the seasonal rarities already mentioned the Spit has also hosted Blue Grosbeak and Swainson's Warbler and has the distinction of being the location for the first and only records of two bird species in Ontario. These two species are Common Ringed Plover (from Eurasia; Prior 2018) and Lesser Goldfinch (from extreme western North America; Frazer 1984).

Birding at the Spit

The Baselands

In my opinion, the Baselands is the top birding spot at the Spit. In terms of accessibility, variety of species, and number of birds, it is difficult to beat. There is a diversity of habitats: wet woods, marsh, wet and dry meadows, and grasslands, which add to the variety of species that may be encountered here. The geographic location of this area also acts as a migrant trap. Birds that follow the shorelines of Lake Ontario are funneled here and find a welcoming oasis among the concrete and asphalt of the city.

Cells 1, 2, and 3

Cell 1 wetland is the largest established marsh area at the Spit. It attracts a variety of marsh birds, as well as migrating waterfowl, songbirds, and shorebirds.

Cell 2 wetland was recently created and vegetation is currently establishing, lending the area to large muddy flats that provide ideal habitat for a variety of migrating shorebirds. This was where the previously mentioned Common Ringed Plover spent several days in August 2016.

Cell 3 is an active confined disposal facility with an expected lifespan of 30 to 50 years. It is a very deep and large area of water and provides an excellent sheltered area for waterfowl in spring and fall and particularly winter, provided it hasn't frozen over.

Peninsulas

All of the peninsulas at the Spit project northwest from the Spine Road. The Bird Research Station is located at Peninsula D. Access to D is limited during banding operations, as mist nets are set up to trap migrating birds. The station itself provides the opportunity to see bird-banding operations first hand. There is no access to Peninsula A, B, and C from April 1 onward until the end of the breeding season. This helps to protect the nesting colonies of waterbirds from disturbance during this critical phase of their cycle. During non-breeding season, these areas can be good for migrants of all types and provide good views of waterfowl in Embayment A. The waterbird colonies are best experienced at a distance for both the protection of the birds and the observer. Peninsula A is relatively small and can harbour migrants, as well as allow views of the inner bays.

Endikement Road, Outer Shoreline, and Open Waters of Lake Ontario

This entire area provides a unique habitat for species of birds that are uncommon in other areas of the Spit. The relatively open expanse of flat land and construction debris attracts open country birds such as American Pipit, Snow Bunting, Horned Lark, and even Lapland Longspur.

The shoreline attracts many different species of shorebird that prefer this type of habitat. Birds such as Whimbrel, Ruddy Turnstone, Red Knot, and Purple Sandpiper (in late fall) occur. It also provides a great loafing area for gulls in winter and, as well as the more common species, Iceland, Glaucous, and Lesser Black-backed Gulls are seen almost annually.

Lake Ontario itself is a huge body of water and, as such, the Spit provides an excellent opportunity to do a "lake watch" for waterfowl and pelagic birds. In the appropriate season and weather conditions, rarities such as Parasitic Jaeger, Pomarine Jaeger, Western Grebe, Eared Grebe, Pacific Loon, and even Northern Gannet are possible.

Recent bird sightings at the Spit/Tommy Thompson Park can be viewed at eBird Canada (https://ebird.org/canada/hotspots).

Environmental Education and Enjoyment at the Spit

Friends of the Spit published the first-ever checklist of birds of the Spit in 1988. At that time the checklist consisted of 284 species of birds. Checklists, compiled by volunteers working with TRCA staff, were also published in 1998 (297 species), 2006 (302 species), and the most recent checklist, published in 2014, includes 316 species. Since then an additional nine species of birds have been added to the ever-growing record.

Several local nature groups organize guided excursions to the Spit. A few of these include the Toronto Ornithological Club (TOC; http://torontobirding.ca), the Ontario Field Ornithologists (OFO; http://ofo.ca/), and the Toronto Field Naturalists (TFN; https://torontofieldnaturalists.org/).

As an urban wilderness the Spit provides an excellent opportunity for people to learn about and get in touch with the natural environment. TRCA provides a number of nature-related educational programs for all ages. More information about these programs can be found at https://tommythompsonpark.ca/education/.

The Tommy Thompson Park Bird Research Station (TTPBRS; https://www.tommythompsonpark.ca/tommy-thompson-park-bird-research-station/), operated by TRCA, provides an opportunity to see their efforts in action and get close-up views of birds as they are measured and banded. TTPBRS also provides a limited number of opportunities for volunteers.

A Recollection

In closing, I would like to recall my first birding experience at the Spit. I was a novice birder, and it was early October 1986. I was amazed at the number of different species of birds that I saw. I was with a group of "beginning birdwatchers," and as the day wore on and the distance we walked got longer and longer, the size of the group began to get smaller and smaller. We were about to call it a day as we were tired and wet weather was threatening, when we were told that a bird I had never heard of, a Purple Sandpiper, had been seen out by the lighthouse. Feeling adventurous, a very small group of us decided to continue the trek to the lighthouse to see if we could find this intriguing bird. As we approached the lighthouse, the cold October rain began to fall. Undeterred we pressed on and began to scan the rubble and barrier stone at the southern-most tip of the Spit for the bird. After about a half-hour, we finally gave up, hungry, cold, and tired. As we made our way back to the parking lot in the pouring rain, I'll never forget how invigorated I felt and how awed I was by the Spit: this magical place where it felt, and still feels, like any species of bird could show up at any time.

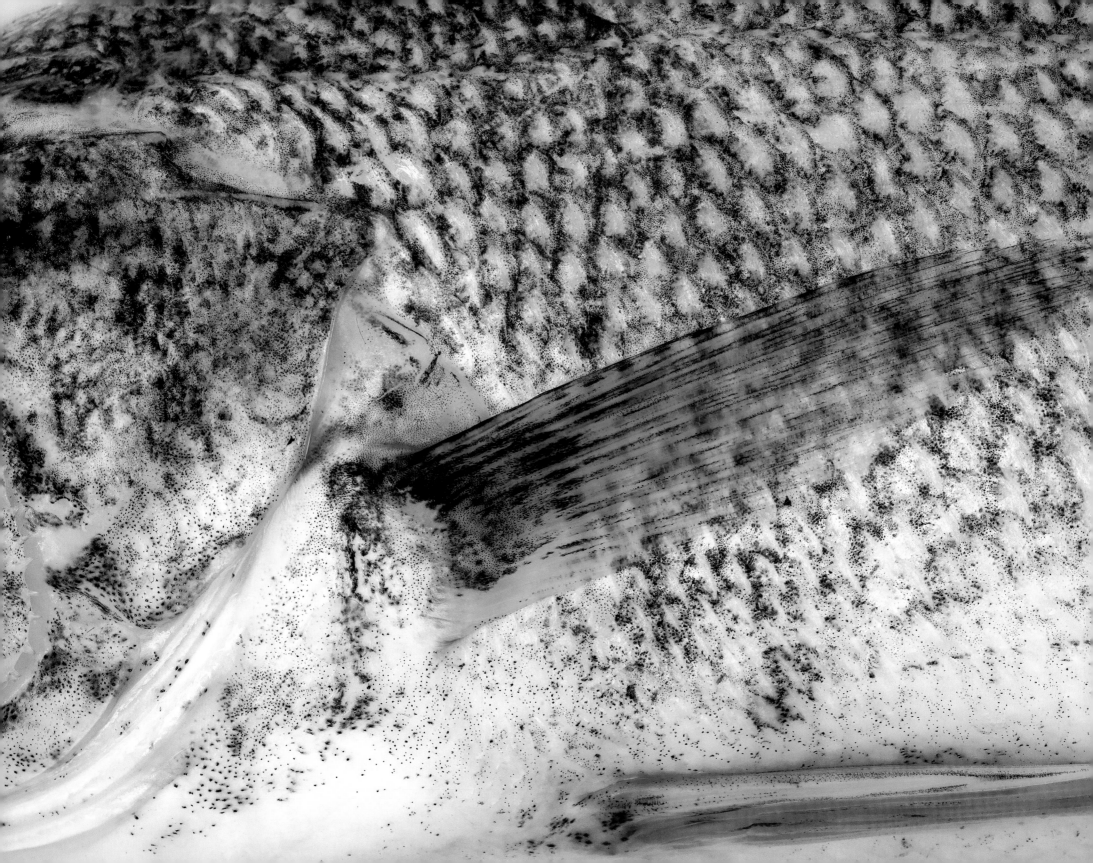

Mammals and Fish

Gord MacPherson

Interviewed by Walter H. Kehm, May 29, 2019

Can you describe Toronto and Region Conservation Authority (TRCA) and its purpose?

The Authority has a significant role to play for cities and regions by filling a void in ecology and watershed planning and design, flood control, and hazard land protection. Municipalities operate with a series of departmental silos, but we take on the responsibility of regional ecological planning, restoration ecology, and sound green design. My task has been to create an environment for consensus building guided by ecological principles. Our work on a variety of environmentally significant areas in the Toronto area, including Tommy Thompson Park, demonstrates how the Authority has worked closely with municipal, provincial, and federal agencies. In each instance, we were able to achieve consensus while creating diverse and sustainable ecological habitats.

In what capacity did you undertake this work?

My position at the Conservation Authority was Associate Director, Restoration Projects that covered the entire Toronto waterfront. A great impetus was the federal legislation in 1988 for "no net loss of habitat." This gave credibility to our habitat restoration work.

How many years have you worked at Tommy Thompson Park and what was the state of the park at that time?

I started at the TRCA in 1982 and began working with Larry Field, eventually taking over his position at Tommy Thompson Park in 1989 as Project Director. [Walter Kehm] had already drafted a master plan with "Conservation by Design" as the guiding principle. He outlined converting the "cells" into wetlands. I was intrigued by the concept of reforming the engineered cells into productive fish and bird habitats and began preparing a Wetlands Master Plan report in 1991. I was amazed, however, that it took 14 years to gain approval.

At the time, the park was an active construction site with grasses and poplars as the predominant species. Hundreds of dump trucks were depositing bricks, concrete rubble, reinforcing bars, and diverse soils every day. Terns and ring-billed gulls were the predominant bird species as they found open ground to develop nests and lay their eggs. The thousands of nests inhabited with chicks were literally one metre from the edge of an active construction road.

Can you describe some of your best memories at the park?

When I began work nobody was involved with ecological restoration on the waterfront. In 1995, we started with a budget of $250,000 from the Ministry of the Environment that allowed a team of three guys to start ecological planning and implementation work. By 2019 the restoration budget grew to approximately $14,000,000 and our staff had increased to 65 women and men. I think this evolution along with the number of restoration projects we have completed are among my major accomplishments.

One of my great memories, and there are many, is the success of the fish habitat creation projects. There was a great deal of skepticism from federal and provincial agencies suggesting that I should not interfere with nature by creating new habitats. There was a misunderstanding of the goals and objectives of the habitat restoration program. Post-war eutrophication led to the increase of species such as carp while native fish populations of bowfin, pike, minnows, and largemouth bass were declining. With the decline of nutrient introduction into the system the native species have rebounded.

Over a two-and-a-half-year period I conducted electro-fishing surveys of more than 250,000 fish and we determined that habitat construction and water quality improvements had increased the number and size of native species while reducing invasive populations. In Cells 1 and 2 we identified their importance for bowfin over-wintering. Embayment C turned out to be the most productive foraging, resting, and spawning area. Great progress was made over time and today habitat restoration is accepted as public policy.

What succession have you seen over the years?

Plants

The master plan used the phrase "Conservation by Design." Through the manipulation of topography and drainage while working with the diverse soils and rubble landscape we helped establish ongoing natural plant succession. There were areas where we inoculated native species such as aspen, pine, and spruce. They were left alone through benign neglect to understand what would happen. The thought was that plants would read the site and establish themselves if it was a fitting environment. If the hardiest survived, they belonged there. I was not concerned about every individual plant but rather what community of plants developed and thrived. There are lessons for parks planning and design because we can now develop a knowledge base for the most useful and successful plants that can thrive without maintenance. This last factor has important economic implications.

A lesson I learned was "Don't plant your garden in rows and count the carrots expecting 100% survival." In restoration work if you plant 100 trees and there is a drought with only 10% survival that is great because we have the toughest species. We don't want wimpy plants.

Fish

I have seen the decline in carp populations and other species but an increase in pike, emerald shiner, minnows, and largemouth bass. The Ministry of Natural Resources are stocking walleye and we can now locate them in the Don River. Through hydro-acoustic surveys we noticed how fish congregated where our structural habitat restoration work had been completed. We tagged many species, and to me it was astounding to see the migration range of fish. Bass travelling to Burlington and walleye to the Bay of Quinte are examples of how far fish will travel. The diminishment of post-war eutrophication has resulted in much improved water quality and the return of healthy fish populations.

Mammals

The development of the mammal populations on the Spit is a fascinating story. I was fascinated with the arrival of the coyotes in the early '90s. They developed a centre of organization and every year four to five pups were born. I don't think people expected them to colonize the area. We began to radio tag them and were amazed to discover their travels. One male migrated to Christian Island via railroad tracks and over the ice. It was found shot there. Others were located in the Barrie area, and cars hit a few.

Today they widely migrate through the city open space systems, the eastern beaches, the Don Valley, other city ravines, headed to distant cities. The coyote has largely displaced the large fox populations that inhabited the Spit.

Beaver have always had a presence because of the abundance of aspen, poplar, and birch trees. It has been interesting to observe how the removal of these trees has resulted in the increase of black locust throughout the site.

Other species such as mink and muskrat have colonized the area, and recently I noticed otter running along the shoreline. Maybe they swam or walked down from the Rouge River Valley. The revival of the mink is an interesting story because it relates to the improvement of the lake water. Mirex is an organochloride that was commercialized as an insecticide and is a bio-accumulative pollutant. It was discharged into Lake Ontario for many years and entered the aquatic food chains, affecting fish and many other species. Mink would eat the contaminated fish and cease to reproduce. With the removal of pollutants the mink population has rebounded and the revival of this species and many other mammals, fish, and birds is a Great Lakes success story. It is a place of constant change and adaptation.

Birds

The Conservation Authority began a bird-banding program in the early 1980s. Using mist netting thousands of birds were caught and released. Frequent flyers include red-eyed vireos, yellow warblers, swallows, red-winged blackbirds, and so many others. A comprehensive list can be found on the TRCA website. An interesting finding for me was the first validated nesting of canvasback ducks in Ontario. Over the years, the original barren construction flats in the 1970s and '80s have become overgrown with vegetation, resulting in the decline of tern, gull, and killdeer populations. However, with the growth of the poplar trees an enormous increase in the black cormorant population has appeared.

Do you have any observations on how the park has grown in the public mind? What are people's favourite activities?

In my view, Tommy Thompson Park is still a "sleeper" as it hasn't yet grown into public consciousness. This is a gradual process, and maybe not a bad thing. I predict it will become increasingly popular, as it is a repository of peace. It is an "urban oasis" providing solace for visitors. It is also an adventure! This new and changing urban wilderness represents money well spent because it provides an escape from daily stresses. People enjoy the waterside trails and remarkably, the straight and wide construction road running down the middle. You can be alone in the crowd!

Do you have thoughts on how the park will continue to evolve?

With the increased urbanization of the city and especially the development of the Port Lands district, thousands of people will be living closer to the park. There may be pressure to create a more typical city park with a variety of amenities for recreation, sport, and cultural activities. This would be a mistake in my view. Interestingly enough, the saving feature may be the park's central and wide access road. It can accommodate large numbers of people, and if they want to find alternative routes there are diverse trail systems to follow. Cyclists in increasing numbers also stay on this paved surface. Because the Spit is car free, a safe and enjoyable recreation experience is provided. It is my hope that the City will buy into enhancing ecologically based natural processes and allow the park to evolve as nature wants it to.

This interview has been edited for length and clarity.

Habitat Projects and Wildlife Management

Andrea Chreston

Habitat Restoration

The Spit has provided an unparalleled opportunity to create and restore habitat on the Toronto waterfront. Building on the natural succession of vegetation that started in the 1970s, the Tommy Thompson Park (TTP) Master Plan outlined a restoration strategy founded on the principle of conservation by design. Coupled with techniques described in the Toronto Waterfront Aquatic Habitat Restoration Strategy, TRCA has created and enhanced more than 60 hectares of aquatic and terrestrial habitat at the Spit since 1995.

Wetland Creation

Traditionally, Confined Disposal Facilities (CDFs) are capped and converted to terrestrial land uses such as parking lots or sports fields. A novel approach, based on a project completed by the U.S. Army Corp Engineers, was taken at TTP, where wetlands were created on top of the capped CDFs at Cell 1, Cell 2, and Triangle Pond. The design sections are included in the chapter "Conservation by Design."

Triangle Pond, approximately one hectare in size, was the original test CDF and was also used as the model for the wetland creation projects. Triangle Pond capping and restoration occurred in 1999, followed by the large-scale projects at Cell 1 (7.7 hectares) from 2003 to 2005 and Cell 2 (9.3 hectares) from 2015 to 2017. In all three instances, a clay or silt cap was placed on top of the contaminated dredge material to biologically and physically isolate it from the surface. The new surficial material was graded to create varying water depths capable of sustaining marsh vegetation, fish, and wildlife habitats. To accomplish this, structural habitat elements were installed, including an abundance of logs, stumps, and stone of various sizes. Emergent and terrestrial areas were planted with thousands of native aquatic, forb, and shrub and tree species. The Cell 1 and Cell 2 wetlands are connected to Lake Ontario by water control structures fitted with fish gates. This feature allows TRCA to manage wetland water levels independent of Lake Ontario, and the gates exclude non-native common carp from entering and causing damage to the wetland habitats.

Common carp (*Cyprinus carpio*) is a species of fish that originates in Asia and was introduced into Lake Ontario in the 1870s. Common carp grow to be very large (up to 22 kilograms), and their foraging and spawning behaviours are detrimental to coastal wetland ecosystems. At TTP the impacts of carp were most obvious in Embayment D; despite its sheltered nature, aquatic vegetation would not thrive in this area. In 2012, TRCA converted the sheltered embayment to a coastal wetland by building a berm to isolate it from the lake; installing a water control structure with a fish gate to maintain native fish access; placing structural habitat features including standing timber, fish cribs; and planting native emergent vegetation. Without the influence of carp, vegetation has thrived in the wetland. These four creation projects resulted in a gain of 24 hectares of wetland on the Toronto waterfront.

Terrestrial Habitat Enhancement

Many projects have been undertaken by TRCA to improve terrestrial habitat. The activities generally focused on the addition of high-quality soil to improve plant viability, the placement of structures such as woody habitat piles to create diverse wildlife opportunities, and planting native wildflowers, grasses, trees, and shrubs. The Toplands are the largest example of terrestrial enhancements at the park. The design included varied topographic height and slope configurations and considered a spectrum of solar aspects from dry, arid conditions to cool, moist, north-facing slopes. This provided for a variety of drainage configurations and accommodated a range of rainfall intensities. Vernal ponds and designed slough depressions connected by drainage channels created the opportunity for diverse vegetation communities to evolve. Habitat structure was added to create microclimate conditions and provide shelter for wildlife. The site was seeded and planted with native species and natural regeneration exceeded expectations, resulting in what is now described as dry meadow, meadow marsh, and thicket. In the Flats area, the same techniques were implemented, but the site is older and has now developed into a treed savannah ecosystem.

Invasive Species Management

Invasive species thrive in disturbed or newly created ecosystems and often outcompete native species, thereby reducing biodiversity. As a new landform with early successional vegetation communities, TTP is highly vulnerable to invasive species. TRCA strategically tracks and manages certain aggressive species to maintain biodiversity. Plants that are of particular concern are dog-strangling vine (*Vincetoxicum rossicum*) and common reed (*Phragmites australis*).

Dog-Strangling Vine – Vincetoxicum rossicum

Dog-strangling vine (DSV) is an invasive meadow plant from Eurasia that was introduced to North America in the 1800s as a garden variety. It grows rapidly and densely with roots that release a chemical that changes the biological composition of the soil, thereby making it less suitable for native species. It is also closely related to milkweed, the family of plants that are essential for monarch butterfly caterpillar survival. Unlike true milkweed, DSV is not a food source for monarch caterpillars; when adults lay eggs on the plant, the caterpillars starve. After being discovered at TTP in the early 2000s, DSV quickly colonized seven hectares of meadow throughout the park. TRCA undertook adaptive management to control its spread and determined that chemical management is the most effective technique. As of 2020, DSV has largely been eliminated and now there are only small patches or individual stems that appear. Ongoing annual treatment is important to ensure the plant is kept at a manageable level.

Common Reed – Phragmites australis

Habitat restoration has been highly successful at TTP; however, the arrival and subsequent invasion of *Phragmites australis* throughout the wetlands has threatened habitat quality. A plant native to Eurasia, it is a strong competitor that reduces the quality and quantity of native wetland species. Its high density of stems crowds out other plants, provides poor habitat and food supplies for wildlife, and lowers water levels through fast growth and rapid transpiration rates.

To protect the restored areas at TTP, TRCA has initiated a *Phragmites* Management Strategy based on best management practices informed by successful programs at other wetlands in Southern Ontario. The goal is to reduce the density and distribution throughout the park using adaptive management and a combination of physical and chemical strategies to restore the emergent aquatic vegetation communities.

Wildlife Management and Monitoring

American Beaver – Castor Canadensis

The Spit has evolved into a refuge that supports diverse communities of wildlife species from all levels of the food chain including insects, mammals, reptiles, amphibians, birds, and fish. While some species are secretive, others leave obvious traces of their presence. One such species is the American beaver that has established a healthy population at TTP. Beavers have built large lodges in many of the wetlands and sheltered embayments, chewing many mature trees and shrubs for construction and as a winter food source. With a finite number of mature trees in the park, TRCA passively manages beaver activity by wrapping the perimeter of trees with wire fence to prevent significant loss.

Double-crested Cormorants – **Phalacrocorax auritus**

Tommy Thompson Park is home to the largest breeding colony of Double-crested Cormorants in North America. Like the American beaver, the cormorant is an ecosystem engineer, as its natural behaviours result in changes to its surrounding habitat. Its acidic excrement limits nutrients available in the soil, reducing the ability of the trees they nest in to absorb water and nutrients required to remain healthy, which ultimately leads to tree mortality. In some ecosystems, cormorants may also impact local fisheries; however, long-term fisheries monitoring by TRCA shows that this colony has not had an impact on the Toronto waterfront.

For these and other reasons, the cormorant is a misunderstood species and has been persecuted. The North American populations have faced serious declines several times in the last 200 years as a result of intensive hunting practices, and most recently from reproductive failures caused by DDT present in the Great Lakes from the '60s to '80s. As DDT has now been banned and cycled out of the ecosystem, cormorants have made a dramatic recovery. However, this is not without conflict with other ecological functions.

In 2007 TRCA worked with an advisory committee to develop a management strategy for cormorants at TTP to address concerns of rapid tree loss at the park, as 24 per cent of the forest had been impacted by cormorants. The TTP Cormorant Management Strategy takes a non-lethal approach to spatially manage the nesting distribution of cormorants by discouraging tree nesting and encouraging ground nesting. The goal of the Strategy is to achieve a balance between the continued existence of a healthy, thriving cormorant colony and the other ecological, educational, scientific, and recreational values of TTP. The Strategy, although labour intensive, has been highly successful – ground nesting has increased from 15 per cent of the population in 2008 to 64 per cent in 2019, and the overall population has more than doubled in this timeframe. More information about the Strategy is available on TRCA's website (www.trca.ca/cormorants).

Tommy Thompson Park Bird Research Station (TTPBRS)

Toronto is located on a convergence of two major bird migratory flyways – the Atlantic and the Mississippi. Millions of individual birds pass through the city every spring and fall as they migrate between northern breeding grounds and tropical winter grounds. Although the best way to track bird populations is to conduct breeding bird surveys (locating all individual nests), this is not feasible for most neotropical migrants as they breed in very remote areas across Canada. Instead, the monitoring occurs during migration when birds funnel through more accessible areas such as Toronto. With the Spit jutting out five kilometres into Lake Ontario, it serves as an essential stopover habitat and is an ideal location to conduct monitoring. TRCA operates the Tommy Thompson Park Bird Research Station on Peninsula D. It is a member of the Canadian Migration Monitoring Network and collects standardized data during spring and fall migration (April 1 to June 9 and August 15 to November 12, respectively). Data collection includes a daily census where all individuals observed within the study are recorded, and bird banding where birds are captured, physically assessed, and fitted with a uniquely numbered aluminum band. The data are submitted to the national bird-banding office and are used to assess long-term population trends, which inform local, regional, and national conservation efforts.

PORTFOLIO III

32
Entrance to the Unassumed
Road, the Neck, 2012

33
Landform in the
Baselands, 2019

following pages

34
Ice formations on
rebar, the Neck, 2019

35
Black Willow tree,
the Neck, 2019

opposite page

36
Cottonwood tree in concrete
rubble, the Neck, 2020

above

37
Cottonwood tree in
winter, the Neck, 2020

38
Russian olive tree,
the Baselands, 2020

following pages

39
Hydro poles on the shore-
line of the Neck, 2019

40
Garlic Mustard,
the Neck, 2020

41
Woodland thicket,
the Baselands, 2020

following pages

42
Wildflowers,
the Baselands, 2019

43
The Hearn Generating
Station, the Baselands, 2019

44
Footpath at the entrance,
the Neck, 2020

45
Black Willow tree,
the Baselands, 2020

46
Concrete rubble and tire,
the Baselands, 2019

47
Chain link fences at the
entrance to the Endikement,
2020

following pages

48
Visitor Centre,
the Neck, 2020

49
Defunct truck entrance
and maintenance yard,
the Neck, 2020

50
Corner of Leslie Street and
Unwin Avenue as seen from
the park entrance, 2020

CYCLIST
STOP
HERE
ON
RED
SIGNAL

PART III: EVOLUTION

People in the Park

Walter H. Kehm

"I go down where the wood drake rests in the beauty on the water and the Great Heron feeds. I come into the peace of wild things who do not tax their lives with the forethought of grief. I come into the presence of still water."

– WENDELL BERRY, *WHAT ARE PEOPLE FOR?* (1990)

In 1956 Rachel Carson wrote *The Sense of Wonder*, revealing the mysteries of the earth, sea, and sky. She was concerned about the future of the planet and hoped to keep alive the miracles of nature for young and old. The inherent appeal of Tommy Thompson Park is its sense of wonder and mystery. People repeatedly return to experience raw nature in a car-free landscape. Meandering through this urban wild is like reading a mystery where the plot continues to unfold with drama and excitement. The park has an inherent sense of wonder.

Today, 55 years later, there is a growing awareness of the fragility of the planet, and more devastatingly, the threats of the extinction of thousands of plant, insect, fish, and animal species. In the span of my lifetime living in the northeast of North America, disease and insect infestations have annihilated elm, chestnut, and ash trees. Beech, oak, and hemlock forests are experiencing severe stress. The Asian pine bark beetle has destroyed the pine forest of British Columbia and Alberta.

There is a growing realization that humankind must reconsider its relationship with the biological world if the planet is to survive. In his book *The Dream of the Earth*, Thomas Berry writes about the need for our re-enchantment with the earth. He states, "[t]his re-enchantment with the earth as a living reality is the condition for our rescue of the earth from the impending destruction that we are imposing on it. To carry this out effectively, we must now, in a sense, reinvent the human species within the community of life species. Our sense of reality and of value must consciously shift from an anthropocentric to a biocentric norm of reference."

In essence, my findings from over 35 years of observation reveal the importance of this urban wild as a place for re-enchantment. There are new miracles revealed every day and every season at the park. Perhaps that is why this park continues to attract ever-growing numbers of people. The park's landscape offers a high level of natural richness through its diversity of plantings, water and sky vistas, landforms, and wild-life. It is where one can have an introduction to the miracles of nature while walking through narrow, meandering paths framed by large trees or through meadows with wild flowers and butterflies or along the lake edges listening to the sound of the waves. Rachel Carson was prescient, since there is "a sense of wonder" in the park.

People are encouraged to explore this natural paradise, and through a process of discovery, something quite beautiful happens. Nature has created a restorative environment where mental fatigue is lessened and moods are lifted. Daily stresses and worries are cast aside as the sounds of crashing waves or the mellow sounds of songbirds become stimuli that allow the mind to transcend into a higher, peaceful realm. The park becomes a happy place with all the restorative aspects for the mind and soul that this world can offer.

The social and mental health importance of the park is realized more and more. Toronto is a rapidly growing, vertical city with an urban core heavily developed with condominiums whose unit size averages between 600 and 700 square feet. These modest dwelling units have a variety of indoor amenities included, but minimal access to outdoor parks and recreation areas. Rooms are small, and to some, claustrophobic. Often, window views face adjacent buildings. It is estimated that by 2024, 31 skyscrapers will be added to these concrete canyons. Is it possible that this removal from nature has created a sense of loss and a desire to reconnect with the biological world? Perhaps the bridge has been crossed when people realize the magic of the natural world and feel a sense of "home" again, as Chief R. Stacey Laforme writes in his closing poem.

Water is the universal symbol of life, and approximately half of the park area is water. Wetland ponds, the triangular pond,

Lighthouse Point, the Outer Harbour embayments and peninsulas allow people to interact with the water edges. The entire eastern, southern, and southwestern outer edges provide expansive views to Lake Ontario. The northwesterly views provide dramatic scenes to the city skyline. The universal appeal of water attracts people to the edges. One is reminded of Henry Thoreau and his 1854 book, *Life in the Woods*, in which he describes his experiences on Walden Pond. Through the changing seasons and the nuances of light reflecting on the rippling water, he describes the pond's changing colours from blue to green. The pond has become earth's eye and the trees that fringe it the slender eyelashes. Thoreau discovered the everyday awe and beauty of secluded cabin living. He attuned himself with the pond's crystal clear waters and the forest's vast majesty. At Tommy Thompson Park, people gravitate to the water edges for rest, reflection, and recreation.

On a recent visit I was walking in the park and met a woman staring over the lake. She looked a bit disoriented, and I stopped to say "hello" and see how she was. Her remark was, "Isn't this heavenly!" I responded with comments about the park's beauty and serenity. She was originally from Toronto but had moved to a sub-Arctic community to find work. At the age of 65, she was told that she had to retire and returned to Toronto. Her voice became subdued when she mentioned that, for two years, she had been seeing a therapist once a week for depression. Her world of infinite spaces in an ever-changing landscape was now limited to a 600-square-foot apartment where she looked into her neighbour's windows and, when looking down, peered into a parking lot. The sun never entered any of her three windows. On arriving at the park, she smelled the pine trees, heard the rustling of the quaking aspen leaves, and arrived at the rippling water's edge. Her response was, "I don't need a therapist anymore. I have found a home!" She was happy again.

This story is typical of many people and families who see Tommy Thompson Park as a safety valve from the daily grind of urban living. The cramped apartment units designed for two people now have families with one or two children. Tommy Thompson Park and many other downtown parks have become backyards for play, sport, and relaxation. These surrogate backyards have become substitutes for those who cannot afford the annual trek to Cottage Country. In his book *Biophilia*, Edward O. Wilson hypothesizes that humankind has an innate need to affiliate with other forms of life. Children love their stuffed animals. The growth of the pet industry is indicative of the need people have for the unmitigated love and affection of a pet. Animals are frequently depicted in popular culture as a means for humans to escape into story and rediscover what it means to love. People gravitate to water to observe the multitude of shorebirds and animal life. They can sit at the water's edge and peer into seemingly limitless space over the lake and feel at home.

When children are brought to Tommy Thompson Park, they are immediately excited by the pebbles on the beach, by the rocks they can climb, and by the puddles they can splash in. Scrap reinforcing bars become armatures to which old bricks with holes can be strung into terracotta necklaces. Pebbles are piled into little forts. Ephemeral block towers are created. Vertical surfaces become TV screens and flat rocks are places to make pancakes. When the creative minds of children are activated, the park becomes an adventure playground. The children's fantasies are realized, and their imaginations are liberated. There is no need for manufactured playground equipment. Nature has provided an abundance of organic opportunities for expression and free play. It is one of the most important aspects of park design: to provide an environment in which people feel happy. The smiling faces of the children and adults are proof of this success. The burdens of city living have been temporarily lifted. In conventional park design, manufactured play objects are statically placed. There is little room to manipulate space and be creative. At Tommy Thompson Park, the opportunities to explore and create are everywhere. It is through these adventures that knowledge of the environment can develop. Children will grow up with wonderful memories of having fun in the park. It has the potential to shape their lives. These memories set the stage for a new generation of nature lovers.

Increasingly, people of all ages have enjoyed jogging, cycling, rollerblading, and skateboarding in the park. The existing construction roads are spacious. As a car-free environment, recreation and fitness enthusiasts easily travel the five kilometres to Lighthouse Point.

In contrast to these recreationalists, the park is a major destination for birdwatchers. It also attracts people who simply want to be in a natural setting without the boundaries enforced by the majority of urban parks. Affordable, green, and accessible, the park draws people in because of its safety and serenity. The ability to experience tranquil adventure and pleasure in an urban wild embodies the essence of the park. The fact that the park is in such demand attests to its popularity. For all the visitors, happiness, enjoyment, and connection is their reward. It is a place to re-create!

Tommy Thompson Park is an example of a global movement to restore balance between the diversity of nature's bounty and society's cultural needs to change and develop the earth. The park opens the dialogue on how we live in harmony with nature. There is a realization that humans are solely responsible for the care of the earth. The future is ours to determine.

Through ecologically based design, new urban wildernesses can be created, offering comfort, shelter, and food for all species that inhabit the planet.

Fig. 33

Fig. 34

Fig. 33
Leslie Street Spit, the Outer Harbour East Headland under construction, 1971. (PortsToronto Archives, PC14/11291)

Fig.34
Robert Smithson, *Spiral Jetty*, 1970. (© 2020 Holt / Smithson Foundation and Dia Art Foundation / Licensed by VAGA at Artists Rights Society (ARS) / Photograph by Gianfranco Gorgoni © Estate of Gianfranco Gorgoni)

Let the Spit Be!!

Robert Burley

In 1970 the artist Robert Smithson embarked on the building of his most famous earthwork, the *Spiral Jetty*, at Rozel Point on the northeastern shore of the Great Salt Lake, Utah. Constructed of mud, salt crystals, and basalt rocks, the monumental structure formed a 1,500-foot-long, 15-foot-wide coil jutting from the shore of the lake. *Spiral Jetty* was typical of the American Land Art Movement, which espoused creating artworks outside commercial galleries, using natural materials that were site-specific. Smithson was reportedly attracted to the Rozel Point site because of its stark anti-pastoral beauty, and, less predictably, a nearby cluster of industrial remnants from the nearby Golden Spike National Historic Site, as well as an old pier and a few abandoned oil rigs. The contradiction made sense. The sculpture sprang from a confluence of Smithson's widespread interests: the environment, geology, and history. In the myriad of essays and books written on the subject of the *Spiral Jetty*, you can read about its relationship to the modern environmental movement and its ties to universal motifs expressed across time and the cosmos. The spiral form, for instance, can be found in the vestiges of ancient civilizations, in galaxies and nebulae in outer space, or natural forces on our own planet such as whirlpools and tornadoes. Smithson himself wrote: "I like landscapes that suggest prehistory. As an artist it is interesting to take on a persona of a geological agent and actually become part of that process rather than overcome it." The *Spiral Jetty* accomplishes just that. It's a man-made adjunct to a piece of natural landscape, as mutable as its setting is to the whims of water levels and erosion, the face of nature itself. And not simply just as mutable but just as unpredictable. "The route to the site is very indeterminate,"

Smithson added. "It's important because it [the access] is an abyss between the abstraction and the site; a kind of oblivion."

In the same year, 1970, that Robert Smithson began moving boulders and earth in Utah, a similar landform was taking shape on the waterfront of the City of Toronto. Like the *Spiral Jetty*, it was constructed mostly of dirt and rock deposited by dump trucks and bulldozers. Like Smithson's work it extended out into a lake (Lake Ontario in this case) and offered a single-entry point that led to a particular end point. But it was not the brainchild of a human mind, creative or otherwise. In fact, by this time "the Spit," as it was then known, was no longer associated with any practical idea or purpose beyond its function as a repository for the rubble of demolished buildings in the city's downtown core. The Spit was a dump.

So while the *Spiral Jetty* in 1970 was a focal point in an isolated mountainous landscape that would one day be known as one of the seminal artworks of the twentieth century, the Spit was just one more element of Toronto's chaotic industrial waterfront, along with generating stations and holding areas for coal, oil, and salt; public beaches, grassroots sailing clubs, and unmanaged wild areas. And where the *Spiral Jetty* would one day be described as "a convoluted question mark that casts doubt on man's relationship to the land," the Spit in 1970 looked more like a sagging and slightly sad exclamation mark in search of a sentence. In fact, the Spit had originally been intended to frame an active commercial harbour, but that idea was quashed by changes in cargo shipping along the Great Lakes. And so the site joined many other lost North American urban landscapes in the latter part of the twentieth century: detritus left by short-sighted planning decisions, the rise of car culture, and urban sprawl.

It's fascinating to wonder today what Robert Smithson would have made of the Spit if he had seen it in his lifetime. It had, after all, the key quality that defined Smithson's chosen sites – those "disrupted by industry, reckless urbanization, or nature's own devastation." It also satisfied Smithson's idea of an anti-romantic "reverse ruin," literally rising up the way it did from the broken bricks and mortar that once constituted the pre-modernist buildings of downtown Toronto. But the Spit also diverged from the *Spiral Jetty* in a way that made it unique. The *Jetty* was remote, requiring a two-hour drive from Salt Lake City, a trip best-suited for four-wheel drive vehicles, at the end of which there were no bathrooms, food to purchase, fresh water, fuel, or cellphone towers. What was startling about the *Spiral Jetty* was its imposition of human geometry on wilderness. What was startling about the Spit, though, was the metropolis looming over it a five-minute walk away. The Spit was the nature of nature wedded to the nature of the city. It had no inhabitants and no history, but its evolution into a hybrid ecological wonder had started already. And almost no one noticed.

When the world did turn its attention to the Spit, in fact, it brought the standard package of perspectives for its "improvement." First came a government-sponsored scheme for an Aquatic Park, which was met with a lukewarm response, then a call for proposals. One early submission from an auto parts company began with the statement: "Toronto is a great city but parts of it make you sick to see them." The remedy that followed described a 400-acre factory complex that included housing, parks, and a school. Subsequent proposals reflected the conventional view that the Spit – or Tommy Thompson Park, as it had come to be known – was an eyesore, a derelict stretch of land in a prime location, at best a blank slate to be filled in or a neglected stretch of scrub in desperate need of a makeover. Proposals for wave pools, wind farms, a theme park modelled on a nineteenth-century seaside village, a golf acad-

emy, an airport, and, yes, a casino were included in the 50-plus submissions that were received annually by City Council. Time passed, and more time, and on May 10, 1996, a scan of a handwritten note emerged from the fax machine in the offices of the City of Toronto Executive Committee:

I am faxing this note to indicate to the committee that I am strongly against any development of the spit or the base of the spit. There are acres of unused land nearby which has no special environmental use – LET THE SPIT BE!!

It was a sentiment that would have been echoed by one of the handful of perspicacious people who had noticed what was happening on the Spit under the city's collective nose: the force behind the book you're reading, Walter Kehm. As Walter describes in his introductory essay, he had fallen under the spell of the Spit and its unique ecology close to the time Robert Smithson was looking out at Great Salt Lake in Utah and seeing a counter-clockwise spiral in his mind's eye. But it was only in the mid-80s, when it had been finally recognized that the Spit was shaping up to be an "environmentally significant area," and its fate was placed in the hands of the local conservation authority, that Walter was officially recruited to help in its design. His mandate: to alter the site to accommodate the explosion of flora and fauna that was colonizing it. Master plans were drawn up by Walter and his team in 1986 and adopted in 1993.

But while funds were made available to begin this transformation, they did not, remarkably, include money for all the elements we commonly associate with parks: public facilities, parking, grassy playing fields, beaches, or carefully planted promenades lined with trees and flowerbeds. It was determined instead that this new landform would have a dual purpose: On the weekends it would be accessible to the public so they could explore its natural wonders, and during the week it would revert to its long-held role of landfill site accessible only to the dump trucks that began lining up in the early morning. The mantra of "Let the Spit be!!" became a battle cry for a growing constituency of birders, cyclists, and naturalists who had discovered the Spit's off-beat splendour and who began to actively fight off any suggestion about disrupting the natural succession that had taken over. It had taken four decades, but finally, at least on one stretch of the north shore of Lake Ontario, society's idea of what nature should look like had shifted and finally embraced Smithson's idea of "the anti-pastoral" as a phenomenon that might even be, well ... beautiful. Tommy Thompson Park today might be home to birds of all kinds, sunken woods, and meadows of native and non-native plants, but it's also defined by chain link fences, shorelines made up of rebar and concrete slabs, and smokestacks visible from nearby industrial complexes.

In the end, perhaps the greatest genius of the Spit is the thing Robert Smithson called "the dialectical landscape"; it has become a place where the natural and artificial features of the terrain have merged. Hence, today visitors to the park admire the vistas of Lake Ontario while studying how the effects of the water have reshaped the bricks, glass, and concrete forms making up the beach. Or they are mesmerized by the ways that a tangle of rebar and the branches of a mulberry tree have intermingled over time. Ultimately there is an engagement and fascination with the collision of the natural and artificial components in a place that is physically in the city but, in many ways, feels very much outside of it. It can all be traced back to Walter Kehm's original master plan, which was informed by a very deliberate decision to fully embrace patience and time in combination with the unexpected and accidental. This is not to say that Tommy Thompson Park is some kind of fortuitous mistake. No significant imaginative creation is. Rather, its strength lies in how it provides a perfect setting for the tricky *pas de deux* between nature and culture, along with the understanding that every transcendent relationship requires the grace of acceptance. On a spring morning, as the five-kilometre trail to the Spit's lighthouse fills up with joggers, birders, cyclists, and photographers (yours truly among them), it's still possible to hear the mantra of this place sung by a chorus of voices that include people, birds, and all other life forms to be found herein:

"Let the Spit be!!"

Home

Chief R. Stacey Laforme

Trees straining toward the sky,
Water splashing on the shore
All around Mother Earth reclaims the mark of man

Our curse, our failing has been and is that we forget the value, the peace, the love of nature
Yet at one time all held the land in esteem
All knew her value because she was always there providing, nurturing

Yet as man moved away, he lost sight of nature, he lost sight of her value
And because so much of man is part of the earth and so much of the earth is a part of man
That as he moves away he forgets
He loses a small part of who he is

He does not notice, oh he knows something is missing but he does not remember
Yet all man need do is leave the concrete and the steel
Walk to this spot, to nature and he will feel at peace relaxed, comforted, home

This is the connection, this the spirit of home so close yet so far
The thing about home is it is always there always welcoming, always waiting
Never truly gone

Nature was, and continues to be, the inspiration for this book. The first time I found myself wandering on "the Spit" some four decades ago, I was awestruck by the transformative powers of nature. In 2019 I met the botanist Dr. Peter Del Tredici, who was in Toronto for a conference and wanted to experience the landscape. We biked and walked the area, and at the end of the day he asked, "What have you written about it?" After a pause, I sheepishly admitted my documentation was limited to my original designs and drawings. He insisted that I write about the evolution of this accidental wilderness, and this encouragement provided a seed that flowered into this book. I thank you, Peter.

This evolution of thought would not be complete without recognition of my family. My wife, Carol, and sons, Jeff and Gregory, constantly gave me inspiration, support, and love. We've shared many summer days at our rustic Parry Sound cottage, along with my daughter-in-law Heidi and grandsons Quentin and Sebastien, where we all walk gently on the land and swim in the clean waters. Throughout the book's development process my grandson Oliver, whose studies are in graphic design, was an appreciated advisor.

My mother was a lover of nature and an avid gardener of the household. Every windowsill and vacant space was given an honoured place for plants, resulting in my father saying, "We live in a jungle." With gratitude to my Dad, his love of the outdoors, and my brother George, who is a keen environmentalist and land steward in Pittsburgh.

My academic studies were so important, as were two of my teachers, Dr. Svend Heiberg, a Danish Professor of Silviculture, and Prof. Author T. Viertel, Professor of Landscape Architecture at the New York State College of Environmental Design and Forestry at Syracuse University. They both shared their deep knowledge of plants and ecosystems while inspiring me to pursue a future career in landscape architecture.

I want to pay tribute to the Toronto and Region Conservation Authority (TRCA), with whom I have had the privilege to work for over 50 years. The unique mandate of the organization is to protect, enhance, and manage the regional landscape of the City of Toronto. The dedicated staff have protected and added to the quality of Toronto's green, living heritage for the use and enjoyment of people, while protecting the watersheds and managing wildlife habitats. My thanks to my colleague of over 25 years, Gord MacPherson, who, working with his associates, oversaw much of the habitat restoration work on the Spit. I also want to acknowledge Larry Field, who was the Tommy Thompson Park Project Manager when I started the new planning and design process. He carefully administered all aspects of communications and report development while carefully guiding our work through the policy and government approval phases. So many people at the TRCA have provided guidance, specifically Andrea Chreston, Karen MacDonald, Rick Portiss, Kaylin Liznick, Nancy Gaffney, and Gavin Miller. I also want to thank the leaders of the TRCA, Ken Higgs, Bill McLean, Craig Mather, Brian Denney and John MacKenzie, with whom I've had the pleasure to work over many decades.

The role of citizen advocacy has been fundamental to the success of the planning and design process. The Friends of the Spit under the leadership of John Carley have been stewards for the natural environment since the inception of the park and continue to oversee its protection as a unique urban wild place. Their vigilant work continues.

The book would not have been possible without the support and encouragement of Jodi Lewchuk, Acquisitions Editor, Social Sciences, at the University of Toronto Press. During our first meeting she recognized the importance of the book and its possible influences on ecological design, urban planning, and landscape architecture. Jodi and her colleagues have been a delight to work with.

The production of this book was the result of many hands and minds that worked together to meet a very tight deadline. To my co-author and photographer extraordinaire, Robert Burley, I thank you for the many hours of hiking through the park in all seasons and weather conditions. The photographs capture the beauty of the park and speak for themselves. Assembling, formatting, editing, and cataloguing all the materials required the skills of project manager Claire Harvie and designer Cecilia Berkovic, who prepared version after version of the book draft until we reached the point of printing. I must also thank editor Jay Teitel and Robert Burley's assistant, Bahar Kamali, a Ryerson University student who worked tirelessly on image editing.

This book would not have been possible without the generous financial support of Mary and Jim Connacher and their family. Their stewardship of the natural landscape has been exemplified by their ecological restoration efforts in the United States and Canada. They demonstrate how people, through their own efforts, can make a difference to regenerate forests, wetlands, and grasslands and increase wildlife habitat.

I also want to acknowledge support from the Ontario Association of Landscape Architects (OALA), whose members work tirelessly through their art and science to plan, design, and construct green infrastructure throughout Ontario. Their efforts have made significant contributions to the sustainable design of cities, waterfronts, rural environments, and greenbelt systems integrating natural processes with the cultural needs of society.

My heartfelt thanks to Chief R. Stacey Laforme and elder Carolyn King of the Mississauga of the Credit First Nation. The Indigenous spiritual essence of living in harmony with nature has been expressed in Chief LaForme's concluding poem, "Home," which he wrote after visiting and being deeply moved by the wild landscape of the Spit. *Miigwech Chi-miigwech.*

COMPARATIVE PARKS

These photographs of globally significant urban parks have been overlaid with the Tommy Thompson Park plan in white. Each comparison demonstrates the large scale and importance of Toronto's newly created urban wild and illustrates how cities throughout the world can increase wildlife diversity and plan for human recreation and enjoyment through conscious creation. "Accidental wilderness" is possible everywhere.

First Row

Central Park, New York City, USA
High Park, Toronto, Canada
Stanley Park, Vancouver, Canada

Second Row

Bosque De Chapultepec, Mexico City, Mexico
Metropolitan Park, Santiago, Chile
Fairmount Park, Philadelphia, USA

Third Row

Regent's Park, London, UK
Tiergarten, Berlin, Germany
Bois De Boulogne, Paris, France

Fourth Row

Phoenix Park, Dublin, Ireland
Schönbrunn Palace and Gardens, Vienna, Austria
Summer Palace Park, Beijing, China

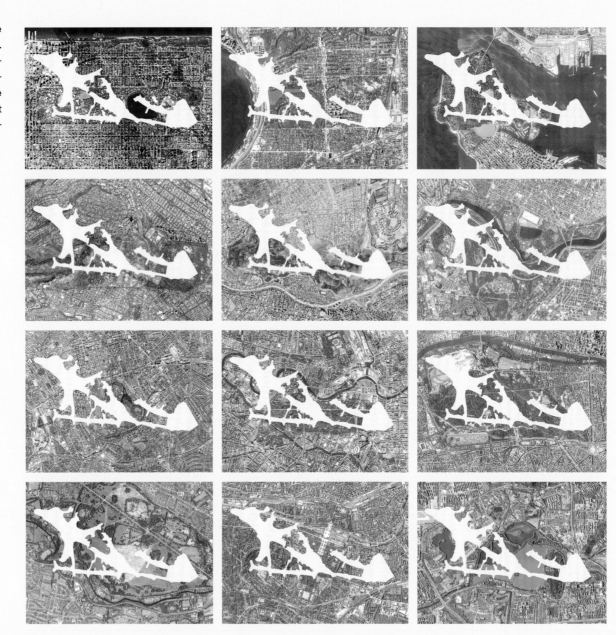

Tommy Thompson Park is one of the best places in the city to enjoy bird watching. In 2000, it was declared an "Important Bird Area" by BirdLife International. The site is globally significant for the numbers of breeding colonial waterbirds and nationally significant for the concentrations of waterfowl that occur during spring and fall migration and in the winter, depending on ice conditions. Also notable are the large concentrations of songbirds during spring and fall migration.

SEASONS (set according to migration patterns)

S   Spring (March 1 – May 31)

SU Summer (June 1 – August 15)

F   Fall (August 16 – November 30)

W   Winter (December 1 – February 28)

ABUNDANCE CODES

A   Accidental: Status based on very few records. Often out of geographic range. Requires documentation.

B   Species has bred at Tommy Thompson Park.

VC Very common: Expected to be observed every day in suitable habitat.

C   Common: Likely to be observed most days in suitable habitat.

U   Uncommon: Not expected daily but observed occasionally, usually in low numbers, except flocking species, which are sometimes numerous.

R   Rare: Present in very low numbers but observed most years.

Migratory birds are only expected to be observed during their migratory period.

	SPECIES	S	SU	F	W
	DUCKS, GEESE, & SWANS				
A	Greater White-fronted Goose				
	Snow Goose	R		R	
	Brant	R		R	
	Cackling Goose	R		R	
B	Canada Goose	VC	VC	VC	VC
B	Mute Swan	VC	VC	VC	VC
	Trumpeter Swan	U	U	U	U
	Tundra Swan	U		R	R
B	Wood Duck	U	U	U	
B	Gadwall	VC	VC	VC	VC
A	Eurasian Wigeon				
	American Wigeon	C		C	C
B	American Black Duck	C	U	C	C
B	Mallard	VC	VC	VC	VC
B	Blue-winged Teal	U		U	
	Northern Shoveler	C		C	
	Northern Pintail	R		U	R
	Green-winged Teal	C		C	R
B	Canvasback	C	C	C	R
B	Redhead	C		C	VC
	Ring-necked Duck	U		U	R
	Greater Scaup	C		VC	VC
	Lesser Scaup	U		U	R
A	King Eider				
	Harlequin Duck			R	R
	Surf Scoter	U		U	U
	White-winged Scoter	C		C	C
	Black Scoter	R		R	R
	Long-tailed Duck	VC		C	VC
	Bufflehead	VC		C	VC
	Common Goldeneye	VC		C	VC
A	Barrow's Goldeneye				
	Hooded Merganser	C	U	C	C
	Common Merganser	C	U	C	VC

	SPECIES	S	SU	F	W
	Red-breasted Merganser	VC		VC	VC
	Ruddy Duck	U		U	
	PARTRIDGES, GROUSE, & TURKEYS				
A B	Ring-necked Pheasant				
A	Ruffed Grouse				
A	Wild Turkey				
	LOONS				
	Red-throated Loon	R		R	
	Common Loon	C	R	C	R
	GREBES				
	Pied-billed Grebe	R		R	
	Horned Grebe	U		U	R
	Red-necked Grebe	C		C	R
A	Eared Grebe				
A	Western Grebe				
	GANNETS				
A	Northern Gannet				
	CORMORANTS				
B	Double-crested Cormorant	VC	VC	VC	R
A	Great Cormorant				
	PELICANS				
A	American White Pelican				
	HERONS & BITTERNS				
	American Bittern	R		R	
	Least Bittern	R			
B	Great Blue Heron	C	C	C	R
B	Great Egret	C	C	C	
A	Snowy Egret				

		SPECIES	S	SU	F	W
		HERONS & BITTERNS (continued)				
A		Tricolored Heron				
A		Cattle Egret				
	B	Green Heron	U	R	U	
	B	Black-crowned Night-Heron	VC	VC	C	
A		Yellow-crowned Night-Heron				
		IBISES & SPOONBILLS				
A		Glossy Ibis				
		VULTURES				
A		Black Vulture				
		Turkey Vulture		U	R	U
		OSPREY				
		Osprey		R	R	
		HAWKS, KITES, & EAGLES				
		Bald Eagle			R	R
		Northern Harrier	C		C	U
		Sharp-shinned Hawk	C	U	C	
		Cooper's Hawk	C	U	C	U
		Northern Goshawk	R		R	R
		Red-shouldered Hawk			R	
		Broad-winged Hawk			R	
		Red-tailed Hawk	U	R	U	C
		Rough-legged Hawk			R	R
A		Golden Eagle				
		RAILS, GALLINULE,S & COOTS				
A		Yellow Rail				
A		King Rail				
	B	Virginia Rail	R		R	
	B	Sora	R		R	
		Common Gallinule	R		R	
		American Coot	U		U	U
		CRANES				
		Sandhill Crane	R			

		SPECIES	S	SU	F	W
		PLOVERS				
		Black-bellied Plover	U		U	U
		American Golden-Plover			R	
		Semipalmated Plover	C	R	C	
A		Piping Plover				
	B	Killdeer	VC	VC	VC	
		STILTS & AVOCETS				
A		Black-necked Stilt				
A		American Avocet				
		SANDPIPERS & PHALAROPES				
	B	Spotted Sandpiper	VC	VC	C	
		Solitary Sandpiper	R			
		Greater Yellowlegs	C		C	
A		Willet				
		Lesser Yellowlegs	C		C	
A		Upland Sandpiper				
		Whimbrel	U		R	
A		Hudsonian Godwit				
		Marbled Godwit				
		Ruddy Turnstone	U		U	
A		Red Knot				
		Sanderling	R		R	
		Semipalmated Sandpiper	U	R	U	
A		Western Sandpiper				
		Least Sandpiper	C	R	C	
		White-rumped Sandpiper	R		R	
A		Baird's Sandpiper				
		Pectoral Sandpiper	R		R	
		Purple Sandpiper			R	R
		Dunlin	C	R	C	
A		Stilt Sandpiper				
A		Buff-breasted Sandpiper				
		Short-billed Dowitcher	U		U	
		Long-billed Dowitcher			R	
		Wilson's Snipe	U	R	U	
	B	American Woodcock	C	C	U	
A	B	Wilson's Phalarope				
A		Red-necked Phalarope				
A		Red Phalarope				

		SPECIES	S	SU	F	W
		GULLS, TERNS, & SKIMMERS				
A		Black-legged Kittiwake				
A		Ivory Gull				
		Bonaparte's Gull	R		R	
A		Black-headed Gull				
A		Little Gull				
A		Laughing Gull				
A		Franklin's Gull				
A		Heermann's Gull				
	B	Ring-billed Gull	VC	VC	VC	VC
A	B	California Gull				
	B	Herring Gull	C	C	C	VC
		Thayer's Gull	R			R
		Iceland Gull	U			U
		Lesser Black-backed Gull				R
		Glaucous Gull	R			R
	B	Great Black-backed Gull	U		U	U
	B	Caspian Tern	C	C	U	
A		Black Tern				
	B	Common Tern	VC	VC	U	
A		Forster's Tern				
		SKUAS, JAEGERS				
A		Pomarine Jaeger				
A		Parasitic Jaeger				
		PIGEONS & DOVES				
	B	Rock Pigeon	C	C	C	C
	B	Mourning Dove	C	C	C	U
		CUCKOOS & ANIS				
		Yellow-billed Cuckoo	R	R	R	
	B	Black-billed Cuckoo	U	U	U	
		TYPICAL OWLS				
A		Eastern Screech-Owl				
		Great Horned Owl	R		U	C
		Snowy Owl	R			R
A		Northern Hawk Owl				
		Barred Owl			R	R
A		Great Gray Owl				

	SPECIES	S	SU	F	W
	Long-eared Owl	R		R	U
	Short-eared Owl	R		R	R
A	Boreal Owl				
	Northern Saw-whet Owl	U		C	U
	GOATSUCKERS				
	Common Nighthawk	R		R	
A	Eastern Whip-poor-will				
	SWIFTS				
	Chimney Swift	C	C	U	
	HUMMINGBIRDS				
	Ruby-throated Hummingbird	U	R	U	
	KINGFISHERS				
B	Belted Kingfisher	C	C	C	
	WOODPECKERS				
A	Red-headed Woodpecker				
	Red-bellied Woodpecker	R		R	
	Yellow-bellied Sapsucker	C		C	
B	Downy Woodpecker	C	C	C	VC
	Hairy Woodpecker	U		U	VC
B	Northern Flicker	C	C	C	R
A	Pileated Woodpecker				
	CARACARAS & FALCONS				
B	American Kestrel	U	U	U	R
	Merlin	U		U	R
A	Gyrfalcon				
	Peregrine Falcon	U	U	U	U
	TYRANT FLYCATCHERS				
	Olive-sided Flycatcher	R		R	
B	Eastern Wood-Pewee	C	C	C	
	Yellow-bellied Flycatcher	U	R	U	
A	Acadian Flycatcher				
	Alder Flycatcher	U	U	U	
B	Willow Flycatcher	VC	VC	C	

	SPECIES	S	SU	F	W
B	Least Flycatcher	C	C	C	
	Eastern Phoebe	C		C	
	Great Crested Flycatcher	U	R	U	
A	Western Kingbird				
B	Eastern Kingbird	VC	VC	C	
	SHRIKES				
A	Loggerhead Shrike				
	Northern Shrike			R	R
	VIREOS				
A	White-eyed Vireo				
A	Yellow-throated Vireo				
	Blue-headed Vireo	U		U	
B	Warbling Vireo	VC	VC	C	
	Philadelphia Vireo	R		R	
	Red-eyed Vireo	C	U	C	
	CROWS & JAYS				
	Blue Jay	C	R	C	
B	American Crow	U	U	U	R
A	Common Raven				
	LARKS				
B	Horned Lark	U		U	R
	SWALLOWS				
	Purple Martin	U	U	U	
B	Tree Swallow	VC	VC	C	
B	Northern Rough-winged Swallow	C	C	C	
B	Bank Swallow	C	C	C	
	Cliff Swallow	U	U	U	
A	Cave Swallow				
B	Barn Swallow	VC	VC	C	
	CHICKADEES & TITMICE				
B	Black-capped Chickadee	C	C	C	VC
A	Boreal Chickadee				
A	Tufted Titmouse				

	SPECIES	S	SU	F	W
	NUTHATCHES				
	Red-breasted Nuthatch	U	R	U	
	White-breasted Nuthatch	U		U	
	CREEPERS				
	Brown Creeper	C		C	R
	WRENS				
B	House Wren	U	U	U	
	Winter Wren	C		C	
A	Sedge Wren				
A	Marsh Wren				
A	Carolina Wren				
	GNATCATCHERS				
B	Blue-gray Gnatcatcher	C	C	R	
	KINGLETS				
	Golden-crowned Kinglet	C		C	R
	Ruby-crowned Kinglet	C		C	
	THRUSHES				
	Eastern Bluebird	U		U	
A	Townsend's Solitaire				
	Veery	U	R	U	
	Gray-cheeked Thrush	U	R	U	
B	Swainson's Thrush	C	U	C	
	Hermit Thrush	C	R	C	
	Wood Thrush	U		U	
B	American Robin	VC	VC	VC	R
A	Varied Thrush				
	MOCKINGBIRDS & THRASHERS				
B	Gray Catbird	C	C	C	
	Northern Mockingbird	C	C	C	C
B	Brown Thrasher	C	U	U	
	STARLINGS				
B	European Starling	VC	VC	VC	C

	SPECIES	S	SU	F	W
	PIPITS				
	American Pipit	U		U	
	WAXWINGS				
A	Bohemian Waxwing				
B	Cedar Waxwing	C		C	C
	LONGSPURS & SNOW BUNTINGS				
	Lapland Longspur	R		R	
	Snow Bunting	U		U	U
	WOOD-WARBLERS				
	Ovenbird	C		C	
A	Worm-eating Warbler				
A	Louisiana Waterthrush				
	Northern Waterthrush	U	R	U	
	Golden-winged Warbler	R		R	
	Blue-winged Warbler	R		R	
	Black-and-white Warbler	U		U	
A	Prothonotary Warbler				
	Tennessee Warbler	U		U	
	Orange-crowned Warbler	R		R	
	Nashville Warbler	C		C	
	Connecticut Warbler	R			
	Mourning Warbler	U		U	
A	Kentucky Warbler				
B	Common Yellowthroat	C	U	C	
A	Hooded Warbler				
	American Redstart	C		C	
A	Kirtland's Warbler				
	Cape May Warbler	U		U	
A	Cerulean Warbler				
	Northern Parula	U		U	
	Magnolia Warbler	C		C	
	Bay-breasted Warbler	U		U	
	Blackburnian Warbler	U		U	
B	Yellow Warbler	VC	VC	U	
	Chestnut-sided Warbler	C		C	
	Blackpoll Warbler	C	R	C	
	Black-throated Blue Warbler	C		C	
	Palm Warbler	C		C	
	Pine Warbler	R		R	

	SPECIES	S	SU	F	W
	Yellow-rumped Warbler	VC	R	VC	
A	Yellow-throated Warbler				
A	Prairie Warbler				
	Black-throated Green Warbler	C		C	
	Canada Warbler	U		U	
	Wilson's Warbler	C		C	
A	Yellow-breasted Chat				
	SPARROWS				
	Eastern Towhee	C		U	
	American Tree Sparrow	C		C	VC
	Chipping Sparrow	U		U	
A	Clay-colored Sparrow				
	Field Sparrow	U		R	
A	Vesper Sparrow				
A	Lark Sparrow				
B	Savannah Sparrow	C		C	U
A	Grasshopper Sparrow				
A	Henslow's Sparrow				
A	Le Conte's Sparrow				
A	Nelson's Sparrow				
	Fox Sparrow	U		U	
B	Song Sparrow	VC	VC	VC	C
	Lincoln's Sparrow	U		U	
	Swamp Sparrow	C		U	R
	White-throated Sparrow	VC		VC	R
	White-crowned Sparrow	C		C	
	Dark-eyed Junco	C		C	U
	CARDINALS & ALLIES				
A	Summer Tanager				
	Scarlet Tanager	U		U	
B	Northern Cardinal	VC	VC	VC	C
	Rose-breasted Grosbeak	U		U	
A	Blue Grosbeak				
	Indigo Bunting	U		U	
A	Dickcissel				
	BLACKBIRDS				
	Bobolink	U		U	
B	Red-winged Blackbird	VC	VC	VC	
B	Eastern Meadowlark	C	U	R	

	SPECIES	S	SU	F	W
A	Yellow-headed Blackbird				
	Rusty Blackbird	U		U	
A	Brewer's Blackbird				
B	Common Grackle	VC	VC	C	
B	Brown-headed Cowbird	VC	C	U	
B	Orchard Oriole	U	U		
B	Baltimore Oriole	VC	VC	C	
	FINCHES				
A	Pine Grosbeak				
	Purple Finch	R		U	
B	House Finch	C	C	U	R
A	Red Crossbill				
	White-winged Crossbill				R
	Common Redpoll	U		U	U
A	Hoary Redpoll				
	Pine Siskin			U	
A	Lesser Goldfinch				
B	American Goldfinch	VC	VC	VC	U
A	Evening Grosbeak				
	OLD WORLD SPARROWS				
B	House Sparrow	VC	VC	VC	VC

As of June 2020, 325 species of birds have been sighted at the Spit. Since the publication of the fourth edition checklist in 2014, ten new species have been sighted, and one species (Thayer's Gull) has been removed from the list as it is no longer regarded as a separate species. The new species added are Fish Crow, Swainson's Warbler, Ross's Goose, Common Ringed Plover, Willow Ptarmigan, Brown Pelican, Fork-tailed Flycatcher, Pacific Loon, Arctic Tern, and Common Ground Dove.

ACORACEAE

Acorus americanus – Sweet flag

ADOXACEAE

Sambucus canadensis – Common elderberry
Sambucus racemosa ssp. *pubens* – Red-berried elder
Viburnum lentago – Nannyberry
Viburnum opulus ssp. *opulus* – European highbush cranberry
Viburnum opulus ssp. *trilobum* –
　　　　American highbush cranberry
Viburnum recognitum – Southern arrow-wood

ALISMATACEAE

Alisma triviale – Water-plantain
Sagittaria latifolia – Common arrowhead

AMARANTHACEAE

Amaranthus albus – Tumbleweed
Amaranthus blitoides – Prostrate pigweed
Amaranthus powellii – Powell's pigweed
Amaranthus retroflexus – Red-root pigweed
Atriplex prostrata – Spreading orache
Bassia scoparia – Ragweed
Celosia argentea – Cockscomb
Chenopodiastrum simplex – Maple-leaved goosefoot
Chenopodium album – Lamb's quarters
Cycloloma atriplicifolium – Winged pigweed
Oxybasis glauca ssp. *glauca* – Oak-leaved goosefoot
Oxybasis rubra var. *rubra* – Red goosefoot
Salsola tragus – Russian thistle

AMARYLLIDACEAE

Allium schoenoprasum – Chives

ANACARDIACEAE

Rhus aromatica – Fragrant sumach
Rhus typhina – Staghorn sumach
Toxicodendron radicans var. *rydbergii* –
　　　　Poison ivy (shrub form)

APIACEAE

Aegopodium podagraria – Goutweed
Angelica atropurpurea – Angelica
Cicuta bulbifera – Bulb-bearing water-hemlock
Cicuta maculata – Spotted water-hemlock
Daucus carota – Queen Anne's lace
Pastinaca sativa – Wild parsnip
Torilis japonica – Hedge-parsley

APOCYNACEAE

Apocynum andosaemifolium – Spreading dogbane
Apocynum cannabinum – Hemp dogbane
Apocynum cannabinum var. *hypericifolium* –
　　　　Clasping-leaved hemp dogbane
Aponcynum × floribundum – Intermediate dogbane
Asclepias incarnata ssp. *incarnata* – Swamp milkweed
Asclepias syriaca – Common milkweed
Vincetoxicum rossicum – Dog-strangling vine

ARACEAE

Lemna minor – Common duckweed
Lemna trisulca – Star duckweed
Lemna turionifera – Turion duckweed
Spirodela polyrhiza – Greater duckweed

ASPARAGACEAE

Asparagus officinalis – Asparagus
Convallaria majalis – Lily-of-the-valley
Maianthemum stellatum – Starry false Solomon's seal
Yucca flaccida – Soft-leaved yucca

ASTERACEAE

Achillea borealis var. *borealis* – Woolly yarrow
Ageratina altissima var. *altissima* – White snakeroot
Ageratum houstonianum – Garden ageratum
Ambrosia artemisiifolia – Common ragweed
Ambrosia trifida – Giant ragweed
Anaphalis margaritacea – Pearly everlasting
Antennaria howellii ssp. *howellii* – Howell's pussytoes

Anthemis arvensis – Corn-chamomile
Anthemis cotula – Stinking mayweed
Arctium lappa – Great burdock
Arctium minus – Common burdock
Artemisia biennis – Biennial wormwood
Artemisia campestris ssp. *caudata* – Beach wormwood
Artemisia vulgaris – Common mugwort
Bidens cernua – Nodding bur-marigold
Bidens frondosa – Common beggar's-ticks
Bidens tripartita – Three-parted beggar's-ticks
Calendula officinalis – Pot-marigold
Carduus acanthoides – Plumeless thistle
Carduus nutans ssp. *nutans* – Nodding thistle
Centaurea jacea – Brown knapweed
Centaurea stoebe ssp. *micranthos* – Spotted knapweed
Cichorium intybus – Chicory
Cirsium arvense – Creeping thistle
Coreopsis lanceolata – Lanced-leaved coreopsis
Cosmos bipinnatus – Cosmos
Crepis tectorum – Narrow-leaved hawk's beard
Erigeron annuus – Daisy fleabane
Erigeron canadensis – Horse-weed
Erigeron philadelphicus var. *philadelphicus* –
　　　　Philadelphia fleabane
Eupatorium perfoliatum – Boneset
Euthamia graminifolia – Grass-leaved goldenrod
Eutrochium maculatum var. *maculatum* –
　　　　Spotted Joe-Pye weed
Filago vulgaris – Common cotton-rose
Gaillardia aristata – Blanket-flower
Galinsoga parviflora – Small-flowered galinsoga
Galinsoga quadriradiata – Hairy galinsoga
Gnaphalium uliginosum – Low cudweed
Helianthus annuus – Common sunflower
Helianthus divaricatus – Woodland sunflower
Helianthus tuberosus – Jerusalem artichoke
Hypochaeris radicata – Cat's ear
Inula helenium – Elecampane
Lactuca canadensis – Wild lettuce

Lactuca serriola – Prickly lettuce
Leucanthemum vulgare – Ox-eye daisy
Matricaria discoidea – Pineappleweed
Pilosella aurantiaca – Orange hawkweed
Pilosella caespitosa – Yellow hawkweed
Pilosella officinarum – Mouse-ear hawkweed
Pilosella piloselloides – Smooth yellow hawkweed
Philosella × floribunda – Smoothish hawkweed
Ratibida pinnata – Grey-headed coneflower
Rudbeckia hirta – Black-eyed Susan
Senecio viscosus – Sticky groundsel
Senecio vulgaris – Common groundsel
Solidago altissima – Tall goldenrod
Solidago canadensis var. *canadensis* – Canada goldenrod
Solidago gigantea – Late goldenrod
Solidago nemoralis – Grey goldenrod
Sonchus arvensis ssp. *arvensis* –
      Glandular perennial sow-thistle
Sonchus arvensis ssp. *uliginosus* –
      Smooth perennial sow-thistle
Sonchus asper – Spiny sow-thistle
Sonchus oleraceus – Annual sow-thistle
Symphyotrichum ciliatum – Rayless aster
Symphyotrichum ericoides – Heath aster
Symphyotrichum lanceolatum – Panicled aster
Symphyotrichum lateriflorum – Calico aster
Symphyotrichum novae-angliae – New England aster
Symphyotrichum urophyllum – Arrow-leaved aster
Symphyotrichum × amethystinum – Amethyst aster
Tanacetum parthenium – Feverfew
Tanacetum vulgare – Tansy
Taraxacum officinale – Dandelion
Tragopogon dubius – Lemon-yellow goat's beard
Tragapogon porrifolius – Salsify
Tragapogon pratensis – Meadow goat's beard
Tussilago farfara – Coltsfoot
Xanthium strumarium – Clotbur

BALSAMINACEAE

Impatiens capensis – Orange touch-me-not

BETULACEAE

Alnus glutinosa – European alder

Alnus glutinosa × incana ssp. *rugosa* –
      European speckled alder
Alnus incana ssp. *rugosa* – Speckled alder
Betula papyrifera – Paper birch
Betula pendula – European white birch

BORAGINACEAE

Cynoglossum officinale – Hound's tongue
Echium vulgare – Viper's bugloss
Hydrophyllum virginianum – Virginia waterleaf
Lithospermum officinale – Eurasian gromwell
Myosotis scorpioides – True forget-me-not
Symphytum officinale – Common comfrey

BRASSICACEAE

Alliaria petiolata – Garlic mustard
Armoracia rusticana – Horse-radish
Barbarea vulgaris – Winter cress
Berteroa incana – Hoary alyssum
Cakile edentula – Sea-rocket
Camelina microcarpa – Small-seeded false flax
Capsella bursa-pastoris – Shepherd's purse
Descurainia sophia – Flixweed
Diplotaxis muralis – Wall rocket
Diplotaxis tenuifolia – Slender-leaved wall rocket
Erucastrum gallicum – Dog mustard
Erysimum cheiranthoides – Wormseed mustard
Hesperis matronalis – Dame's rocket
Lepidium campestre – Field pepper-grass
Lepidium densiflorum – Common pepper-grass
Lepidium ruderale – Roadside pepper-grass
Lepidium virginicum – Virginia pepper-grass
Lobularia maritima – Sweet alyssum
Nasturtium microphyllum – Small-leaved watercress
Rorippa palustris ssp. *hispida* – Hispid marsh grass
Rorippa palustris – Fernald's marsh cress
Sinapsis arvensis – Charlock
Sisymbrium altissimum – Tumble mustard
Sisymbrium officinale – Hedge mustard
Thlaspi arvense – Penny-cress

BUTOMACEAE

Butomus umbellatus – Flowering-rush

CACTACEAE

Opuntia cespitosa – Eastern prickly-pear

CAMPANULACEAE

Campanula aparinoides – Marsh bellflower
Campanula rapunculoides – Creeping bellflower
Lobelia siphilitica – Great blue lobelia

CANNABACEAE

Celtis occidentalis – Hackberry
Humulus japonicus – Japanese hops

CAPRIFOLIACEAE

Dipsacus fullonum – Teasel
Lonicera morrowii – Morrow's honeysuckle
Lonicera tatarica – Tatarian honeysuckle
Lonicera × bella – Shrub honeysuckle
Lonicera xylosteum – European fly honeysuckle
Symphoricarpos albus var. *albus* – Eastern snowberry
Symphoricarpos albus var. *laevigatus* –
      Western snowberry
Valeriana officinalis – Common valerian

CARYOPHYLLACEAE

Arenaria serpyllifolia – Thyme-leaved sandwort
Cerastium fontanum – Mouse-ear chickweed
Saponaria officinalis – Bouncingbet
Silene antirrhina – Sleepy catchfly
Silene csereii – Lesser bladder campion
Silene latifolia – Evening lychnis
Silene noctiflora – Night-flowering catchfly
Silene vulgaris – Bladder campion
Spergularia salina – Salt-marsh sand spurrey
Stellaria media – Common chickweed

CELASTRACEAE

Celastrus orbiculatus – Oriental bittersweet

CERATOPHYLLACEAE

Ceratophyllum demersum – Coontail

CLEOMACEAE

Tarenaya hassleriana – Spiderflower

COMMELINACEAE
Commelina communis – Asiatic dayflower

CONVOLVULACEAE
Calystegia sepium ssp. *americana* –
    Pink hedge bindweed
Convovulus arvensis – Field bindweed
Cuscuta gronovii – Swamp dodder
Ipomoea purpurea – Common morning-glory

CORNACEAE
Cornus obliqua – Silky dogwood
Cornus racemosa – Grey dogwood
Cornus sericea – Red osier dogwood

CRASSULACEAE
Hylotelephium tetephium – Live-forever
Sedum acre – Mossy stonecrop

CUCURBITACEAE
Citrullus lanatus – Watermelon
Cucumis sativus – Cucumber
Echinocystis lobata – Wild cucumber

CUPRESSACEAE
Juniperus chinensis – Chinese juniper
Juniperus communis var. *depressa* –
    Common juniper
Juniperus virginiana – Red cedar
Thuja occidentalis – White cedar

CYPERACEAE
Bolboschoenus fluviatilis – River bulrush
Carex aquatilis – Water sedge
Carex aurea – Golden-fruited sedge
Carex bebbii – Bebb's sedge
Carex blanda – Common wood sedge
Carex cristatella – Crested sedge
Carex granularis – Meadow sedge
Carex hystericina – Porcupine sedge
Carex lacustris – Lake-bank sedge
Carex molesta – Troublesome sedge
Carex muehlenbergii – Muhlenberg's sedge

Carex pellita – Woolly sedge
Carex spicata – Spiked sedge
Carex stricta – Tussock sedge
Carex vulpinoidea – Fox sedge
Cyperus bipartitus – Umbrella sedge
Cyperus engelmanii – Engelmann's flatsedge
Cyperus erythrorhizos – Red-rooted umbrella-sedge
Cyperus esculentus – Yellow nut-sedge
Cyperus fuscus – Brown umbrella-sedge
Cyperus odoratus – Fragrant umbrella-sedge
Eleocharis acicularis – Needle spike-rush
Eleocharis erythropoda – Creeping spike-rush
Schoenoplectus acutus – Hard-stemmed bulrush
Schoenoplectus pungens – Three-square
Schoenoplectus tabernaemontani –
    Soft-stemmed rush
Scirpus atrovirens – Black-fruited bulrush
Scirpus cyperinus – Woolly bulrush
Scirpus microcarpus – Barber-pole bulrush
Scirpus pendulus – Drooping bulrush

DRYOPTERIDACEAE
Dryopteris cristata – Crested wood fern

ELAEAGNACEAE
Elaeagnus angustifolia – Russian olive
Elaeagnus commutata – Silver-berry
Elaeagnus umbellata – Autumn olive
Shepherdia argentea – Silver buffalo-berry

EQUISETACEAE
Equisetum arvense – Field horsetail
Equisetum hyemale ssp. *affine* – Scouring-rush
Equisetum variegatum – Variegated scouring-rush
Equisetum × nelsonii – Nelson's horsetail

ERICACEAE
Pyrola asarifolia – Pink pyrola

EUPHORBIACEAE
Acalypha rhomboidea – Three-seeded mercury
Euphorbia glyptosperma – Ridge-seeded spurge
Euphorbia helioscopia – Sun spurge

Euphorbia maculata – Spotted spurge
Euphorbia marginata – Snow-on-the-mountain
Euphorbia peplus – Petty spurge
Euphorbia polygonifolia – Seaside spurge
Euphorbia serpillifolia – Thyme-leaved spurge
Euphorbia vermiculata – Hairy spurge

FABACEAE
Desmodium canadense – Showy tick-trefoil
Lathyrus odoratus – Sweet pea
Lathyrus palustris – Marsh vetchling
Lotus corniculatus – Bird's foot trefoil
Medicago lupulina – Black medick
Medicago sativa – Alfalfa
Meliotus albus – White sweet clover
Meliotus officinalis – Yellow sweet clover
Robinia pseudoacacia – Black locust
Securigera varia – Crown vetch
Trifolium campestre – Large hop-clover
Trifolium fragiferum – Strawberry clover
Trifolium hybridum – Alsike clover
Trifolum pratense – Red clover
Trofolium repens – White clover
Vicia cracca – Cow vetch
Quercus robur – English oak
Quercus rubra – Red oak

GENTIANACEAE
Centaurium pulchellum – Branching centaury
Gentianopsis crinita – Fringed gentian

GERANIACEAE
Erodium cicutarium – Common stork's-bill

HALORAGACEAE
Myriophyllum sibiricum – Northern watermilfoil
Myriophyllum spicatum – Eurasian watermilfoil

HYDROCHARITACEAE
Elodea canadensis – Common water-weed
Elodea nuttallii – Nuttall's water-weed
Najas flexilis – Bushy naiad
Vallisneria americana – Tape-grass

HYPERICACEAE
Hypericum perforatum – Common St. John's-wort

IRIDACEAE
Iris pseudacorus – Yellow flag
Iris virginica var. *shrevei* – Southern blue flag
Iris × germanica – Garden iris

JUGLANDACEAE
Juglans cinerea – Butternut
Juglans nigra – Black walnut

JUNCACEAE
Juncus alpinoarticulatus – Richardson's rush
Juncus articulatus – Jointed rush
Juncus balticus ssp. *littoralis* – Baltic rush
Juncus bufonius – Toad rush
Juncus compressus – Round-fruited rush
Juncus dudleyi – Dudley's rush
Juncus effusus – Soft rush
Juncus nodosus – Knotted rush
Juncus tenuis – Path rush
Juncus torreyi – Path rush

LAMIACEAE
Ajuga reptans – Common bugle
Dracocephalum parviflorum – American dragonhead
Glechoma hederacea – Creeping Charlie
Leonurus cardiaca – Motherwort
Lycopus americanus – American water-horehound
Lycopus americanus × europaeus –
      Hybrid water-horehound
Lycopus europaeus – European water-horehound
Mentha canadensis – Wild mint
Mentha spicata – Spearmint
Mentha × gentilis – Red mint
Mentha × piperita – Peppermint
Mentha × verticillata – Hybrid mint
Monarda fistulosa – Wild bergamot
Nepeta cataria – Catnip
Origanum vulgare – Wild oregano
Physostegia virginiana – False dragonhead
Prunella vulgaris ssp. *lanceolata* – Heal-all (native)

Scutellaria galericulata – Common skullcap
Scutellaria lateriflora – Mad-dog skullcap
Stachys palustris – Marsh hedge-nettle
Teucrium canadense – Wood-sage
Thymus praecox ssp. *brittanicus* – Creeping thyme

LILIACEAE
Tulipa × hybrida – Garden tulip

LINDERNIACEAE
Lindernia dubia – False pimpernel

LYTHRACEAE
Lythrum salicaria – Purple loosestrife

MALVACEAE
Abutilon theophrasti – Velvet-leaf
Alcea rosea – Hollyhock
Hibiscus trionum – Flower-of-an-hour
Malva moschata – Musk mallow
Malva neglecta – Common mallow
Malva pusilla – Round-leaved mallow
Tilia americana – Basswood
Tilia cordata – Little-leaf linden

MOLLUGINACEAE
Mollugo verticillata – Carpet-weed

MORACEAE
Morus alba – White mulberry

NYCTAGINACEAE
Mirabilis nyctaginea – Wild four o'clock

NYMPHAEACEAE
Nuphar variegata – Bullhead lily
Nymphaea odorata ssp. *tuberosa* –
      Tuberous water-lily

OLEACEAE
Forsythia viridissima – Forsythia
Fraxinus americana – White ash
Fraxinus pennsylvanica – Red ash

ONAGRACEAE
Epilobium ciliatum – Sticky willow-herb
Epilobium coloratum – Purple-leaved willow-herb
Epilobium hirsutum – European willow-herb
Oenothera biennis – Common evening-primrose

ONOCLEACEAE
Matteuccia struthiopteris var. *pensylvanica* – Ostrich fern
Onoclea sensibilis – Sensitive fern

OPHIOGLOSSACEAE
Botrypus virginianus – Rattlesnake fern

ORCHIDACEAE
Cypripedium parviflorum var. *makasin* –
      Smaller yellow lady's slipper
Cypripedium reginae – Showy lady's slipper
Epipactis helleborine – Helleborine
Liparis loeselii – Loesel's twayblade
Plantathera aquilonis – Tall northern green orchid
Spiranthes incurva – Nodding ladies' tresses
Spiranthus magnicamporum – Great Plains ladies' tresses

OROBANCHACEAE
Agalinis tenuifolia – Slender gerardia

OXALIDACEAE
Oxalis stricta – Common yellow wood-sorrel

PAPAVERACEAE
Chelidonium majus – Celandine
Papaver dubium – Smooth-fruited poppy
Papaver orientale – Oriental poppy
Papaver somniferum – Opium poppy

PHRYMACEAE
Mimulus ringens – Square-stemmed monkey-flower

PINACEAE
Larix laricina – Tamarack
Picea abies – Norway spruce
Picea glauca – White spruce
Pinus nigra – Austrian pine

Pinus resinosa – Red pine
Pinus strobus – White pine
Pinus sylvestris – Scots pine

PLANTAGINACEAE

Antirrhinum majus – Snapdragon
Chaenorrhinum minus – Dwarf snapdragon
Chelone glabra – Turtlehead
Linaria vulgaris – Butter-and-eggs
Penstemon digitalis – Foxglove beard-tongue
Plantago arenaria – Sand plantain
Plantago lanceolata – English plantain
Plantago major – Common plantain
Veronica anagallis-aquatica – Water speedwell
Veronica longifolia – Long-leaved speedwell
Veronica serpyllifolia – Thyme-leaved speedwell

POACEAE

Agropyron cristatum – Crested wheat grass
Agrostis gigantea – Redtop
Agrostis scabra – Ticklegrass
Agrostis stolonifera – Creeping bent grass
Ammophila breviligulata – Marram grass
Andropogon gerardii – Big bluestem
Avena sativa – Oats
Bouteloua curtipendula – Sideoats grama
Bromus commutatus – Upright chess
Bromus inermis – Smooth brome grass
Bromis tectorum – Downy chess
Calmagrostis canadensis – Canada blue joint
Cenchrus longispinus – Sand-bur
Dactylis glomerata – Orchard grass
Dichanthelium implicatum – Hairy panic grass
Dichanthelium lindheimeri – Lindheimer's panic grass
Digitaria ischaemum – Smooth crab grass
Echinochloa crus-galli – Barnyard grass
Echinochloa muricata var. *microstachya* –
        Small-spiked barnyard grass
Echinochloa muricata – Western barnyard grass
Elymus canadensis – Canada wild rye
Elymus repens – Quack grass
Eragrostis minor – Little love grass
Eragrostis pectinacea – Tufted love grass

Festuca filiformis – Hair fescue
Festuca rubra – Red fescue
Festuca trachyphylla – Hard fescue
Hordeum jubatum – Squirrel-tail barley
Leersia oryzoides – Rice cut grass
Lolium arundinaceum – Tall fescue
Lolium perenne – Perennial rye
Lolium pratense – Meadow fescue
Muhlenbergia mexicana – Common muhly grass
Panicum capillare – Panic grass
Panicum dichotomiflorum – Fall panic grass
Panicum virgatum – Switch grass
Phalaris arundinacea – Reed canary grass
Phalaris canariensis – Canary grass
Phleum pratense – Timothy grass
Phragmites australis – Common reed
Poa annua – Annual bluegrass
Poa compressa – Flat-stemmed bluegrass
Poa nemoralis – Woodland spear grass
Poa palustris – Fowl meadow-grass
Poa pratensis – Kentucky bluegrass
Puccinellia distans – Alkali grass
Schizachyrium scoparium – Little bluestem
Setaria pumila – Yellow foxtail
Setaria viridis – Green foxtail
Sorghastrum nutans – Indian grass
Sporobolus cryptandrus – Sand dropseed
Sporobolus vaginiflorus – Ensheathed dropseed
Triticum aestivum – Wheat
Zea mays – Maize

POLYGONACEAE

Fagopyrum esculentum – Buckwheat
Fallopia convolvulus – Black bindweed
Persicaria hydropiper – Water-pepper
Persicaria lapathifolia – Pale smartweed
Persicaria maculosa – Lady's thumb
Persicaria orientalis – Prince's feather
Persicaria pensylvanica – Pennsylvania smartweed
Polygonum achoreum – Striate knotweed
Polygonum aviculare – Prostrate knotweed
Reynoutria japonica – Japanese knotweed
Reynoutria × bohemica – Hybrid knotweed

Rumex crispus – Curly dock
Rumex fueginus – Golden dock
Rumex obtusifolius – Bitter dock

PONTEDERIACEAE

Heteranthera dubia – Water star-grass

PORTULACACEAE

Portulaca grandiflora – Garden portulaca
Portulaca oleracea – Purslane

POTAMOGETONACEAE

Potamogeton crispus – Curly pondweed
Potamogeton foliosus – Leafy pondweed
Potamogeton richardsonii – Redhead pondweed
Stuckenia pectinata – Sago pondweed
Zannichellia palustris – Horned pondweed

PRIMULACEAE

Lysimachia arvensis – Scarlet pimpernel
Lysimachia ciliata – Fringed loosestrife
Lysimachia thyrsiflora – Tufted loosestrife
Lysimachia vulgaris – Garden loosestrife

RANUNCULACEAE

Anemonastrum canadense – Canada anemone
Anenome virginiana – Common thimbleweed
Aquilegia vulgaris – Garden columbine
Ranunculus acris – Tall buttercup
Ranunculus sceleratus – Cursed buttercup
Thalictrum pubescens – Tall meadow rue

RHAMNACEAE

Frangula alnus – Glossy buckthorn
Rhamnus cathartica – Common buckthorn

ROSACEAE

Agrimonia gryposepala – Agrimony
Amelanchier arborea – Downy serviceberry
Amelanchier interior – Serviceberry complex
Amelanchier laevis – Smooth serviceberry
Aronia melanocarpa – Black choke-berry
Crataegus macracantha – Long-spined hawthorn

Fragaria virginiana – Wild strawberry
Geum aleppicum – Yellow avens
Geum canadense – White avens
Geum laciniatum – Cut-leaved avens
Geum urbanum – Urban avens
Malus pumila – Apple
Physocarpus opulifolius – Ninebark
Potentilla anserina – Silverweed
Potentilla argentea – Silvery cinquefoil
Potentilla inclinata – Intermediate cinquefoil
Potentilla norvegica – Rough cinquefoil
Potentilla recta – Sulphur cinquefoil
Potentilla supina ssp. *paradoxa* – Bushy cinquefoil
Prunus avium – Mazzard cherry
Prunus domestica – Common plum
Prunus pensylvanica – Pin cherry
Prunus persica – Peach
Prunus serotina – Black cherry
Prunus virginiana – Choke cherry
Rosa canina – Dog rose
Rosa rugosa – Rugosa rose
Rubus idaeus ssp. *strigosus* – Wild red raspberry
Rubus occidentalis – Wild black raspberry
Rubus odoratus – Purple-flowering raspberry
Sorbus aucuparia – European mountain-ash
Spiraea alba – Wild spiraea

RUBIACEAE
Galium mollugo – White bedstraw
Galium palustre – Marsh bedstraw
Galium verum – Yellow bedstraw

SALICACEAE
Populus alba – White poplar
Populus balsamifera – Balsam poplar
Populus deltoides – Cottonwood
Populus grandidentata – Large-toothed aspen
Populus tremuloides – Trembling aspen
Populus × *heimburgeri* – Heimburger's poplar

Populus × *jackii* – Jack's poplar
Populus × *rouleauiana* – Rouleau's poplar
Salix alba – White willow
Salix amygdaloides – Peach-leaved willow
Salix bebbiana – Bebb's willow
Salix caprea – Goat willow
Salix cinerea – Grey willow
Salix discolor – Pussy willow
Salix eriocephala – Narrow heart-leaved willow
Salix interior – Sandbar willow
Salix lucida – Shining willow
Salix matsudana – Corkscrew willow
Salix nigra – Black willow
Salix petiolaris – Slender willow
Salix purpurea – Purple-osier willow
Salix × *fragilis* – Crack willow
Salix × *sepulcralis* – Weeping willow

SAPINDACEAE
Acer negundo – Manitoba maple
Acer platanoides – Norway maple
Acer saccharinum – Silver maple
Acer saccharum – Sugar maple
Aesculus hippocastanum – Horse-chestnut

SCROPHULARIACEAE
Verbascum thapsus – Common mullein

SIMAROUBACEAE
Ailanthus altissima – Tree-of-heaven

SOLANACEAE
Datura stramonium – Jimsonweed
Nicotiana longiflora – Long-leaved tobacco
Petunia × *atkinsiana* – Garden petunia
Physalis heterophylla – Clammy ground-cherry
Solanum dulcamara – Bittersweet nightshade
Solanum emulans – American black nightshade
Solanum lycopersicum – Tomato

THELYPTERIDACEAE
Thelypteris palustris var. *pubescens* – Marsh fern

TYPHACEAE
Sparganium eurycarpum – Great bur-reed
Typha angustifolia – Narrow-leaved cattail
Typha latifolia – Broad-leaved cattail
Typha × *glauca* – Hybrid cattail

ULMACEAE
Ulmus americana – White elm
Ulmus glabra – Scotch elm
Ulmus pumila – Siberian elm

URTICACEAE
Boehmeria cylindrica – False nettle
Urtica dioica ssp. *dioica* – European stinging nettle
Urtica dioica ssp. *gracilis* – American stinging nettle
Urtica urens – Dwarf nettle

VERBENACEAE
Verbena bracteata – Creeping vervain
Verbena hastata – Blue vervain
Verbena stricta – Hoary vervain
Verbena urticifolia – White vervain

VIOLACEAE
Viola tricolor – Johnny jump-up

VITACEAE
Vitis riparia – Riverbank grape

XANTHORRHOEACEAE
Hemerocallis fulva – Orange day-lily

Please contact Toronto and Region Conservation Authority
at info@trca.ca for a detailed list of dates of observation and
status for each plant species.

Berry, Wendell. 1990. *What Are People for?* New York: North Point Press.

Canadian Wildlife Service. 2000. "Great Lakes Wetlands Conservation Action Plan Highlights Report, 1997–2000." Toronto: Environment Canada.

Carson, Rachel. 1965. The *Sense of Wonder*. New York: Harper Collins Publishers.

Catling P.M., K.L. McIntosh, and S.M. McKay. 1977. "The Vascular Plants of the Leslie Street Headland." *Ontario Field Biologist* 31 (1): 23–39.

Coady, Glenn, "First Nest Records of Canvasback in Ontario." *Ontario Birds* 18(3): 115-25.

Committee on the Status of Endangered Wildlife in Canada (COSEWIC). 2019. "Species at Risk Public Registry." https://wildlife-species.canada.ca/species-risk-registry/sar/index/default_e.cfm

Dupuis-Désormeaux M., C. Davy, A. Lathrop, E. Followes, A. Ramesbottom, A. Chreston, and S. MacDonald. 2018. "Colonization and Usage of an Artificial Urban Wetland Complex by Freshwater Turtles." *Peer Journal* 6: e5423. https://peerj.com/articles/5423/

Dupuis-Désormeaux, M., Ian Sturdee, Don Johnston, and Paul Xamin. 2017. "First Record of Least Bittern Nesting at Tommy Thompson Park in Toronto, Ontario." *Ontario Birds* 35(3): 146–50.

Environment Canada. 1995. "Habitat Rehabilitation in the Great Lakes: Techniques for Enhancing Biodiversity." August 31.

Eyles, N. 2004. *Toronto Rocks: The Geological Legacy of the Toronto Region*. Markham, ON: Fitzhenry & Whiteside.

Fairfield, George, ed. 1998. *Ashbridge's Bay: An Anthology of Writings by Those Who Knew and Loved Ashbridge's Bay*. Toronto: Toronto Ornithological Club.

Ferko, Ryan. 2014. "Delinquent History: For Sites of Transition." OCAD University Open Research Repository. Dissertation, OCAD University. http://openresearch.ocadu.ca/id/eprint/68

Frazer, Donald M. 1984. "Lesser Goldfinch (*Carduelis psaltria*) at Toronto: Ontario's First Record." *Ontario Birds* 2(3): 120–23.

Friends of the Spit. 1990. *Checklist: Plants of the Leslie Street Spit*. Toronto. Accessed January 28, 2020. https://friendsofthespit.ca/wp-content/uploads/2016/09/FOS-Checklist-Plants-of-the-Leslie-Stree-Spit.pdf.

– 2020. Friends of the Spit. https://friendsofthespit.ca.

Grady, Wayne. 1995. *Toronto the Wild: Field Notes of an Urban Naturalist*. Toronto: Macfarlane, Walter & Ross.

Hammer, Donald A. 1992. *Creating Freshwater Wetlands*. Boca Raton, FL: Lewis Publishers.

Higgins, Verna J., Susan Denzel, and Nancy Fazari. 1992. *Plant Communities of the Leslie Street Spit, A Beginner's Guide*. Toronto: Friends of the Spit.

Jacobs, Jane. 1961. *The Death and Life of Great American Cities*. New York: Random House.

Kalff, S., G. MacPherson, and G. Miller. 1991. *Environmental Audit of the East Bayfront / Port Industrial Area Phase II: Natural Heritage*. Royal Commission on the Future of the Toronto Waterfront, Technical Paper #10.

Kehm, Walter H. 1989. "Tommy Thompson Park: Wetlands Development and Restoration." In Michael J. Bardecki and Nancy E. Patterson, eds., *Wetlands: Inertia or Momentum Conference Proceedings*, Oct. 21–22, 143. Toronto: Federation of Ontario Naturalists.

Kellert, Steven R., and Edward O. Wilson. 1993. The *Biophilia Hypothesis*. Washington, D.C.: Island Press.

Lee, H., W.D. Bakowsky, J. Riley, J. Bowles, M. Puddister, P. Uhlig, and S. McMurray. 1998. *Ecological Land Classification for Southern Ontario: First Approximation and Its Application*. Peterborough: Ontario Ministry of Natural Resources, Southcentral Science Section, Science Development and Transfer Branch.

Metropolitan Toronto and Region Conservation Authority (MTRCA). 1982. *Aquatic Park Environmental Study: 1978–1982*. Toronto: MTRCA.

– 1986a. *Tommy Thompson Park Alternative Concept Plans Phase 1 Information Kit*. Toronto: MTRCA.

– 1985. *Aquatic Park Master Plan Zones*. Toronto: MTRCA.

– 1986b. *Tommy Thompson Park Concept Plan Potential Site Uses*. Toronto: MTRCA.

– 1989. *Tommy Thompson Park Master Plan and Environmental Assessment*. June. Toronto: MTRCA.

– 1992a. "Addendum: Tommy Thompson Park Master Plan and Environmental Assessment." Toronto: MTRCA.

– 1992b. "Capping Proposal for Cell 1 at Tommy Thompson Park." Proposal submitted to Ontario Ministry of the Environment. Toronto: MTRCA.

– 1994. "Wetland Concept Plan – Tommy Thompson Park Disposal Cell 1." Toronto: MTRCA.

NatureServe. 2019. "NatureServe National and Subnational Conservation Status Definition." Accessed May 22, 2020. https://explorer.natureserve.org/AboutTheData/Statuses

Prior, Paul. (2018). "Common Ringed Plover at Tommy Thompson Park: New to Ontario." *Ontario Birds* 36(2): 105–09.

Royal Commission on the Future of the Toronto Waterfront (Crombie Commission). 1992. *Regeneration: Toronto's Waterfront and the Sustainable City: Final Report*. Toronto: Royal Commission on the Future of the Toronto Waterfront.

Temple, P.J. 1980. "Plants of the Leslie Street Headland." *Ontario Field Biologist* 34(1): 19–32.

Toronto and Region Conservation Authority (TRCA). 2017a. "Management of Double-Crested Cormorants at Tommy Thompson Park. 2017 Summary Report." Toronto: TRCA. Accessed January 27,

2020. https://tommythompsonpark.ca/app/
        uploads/2018/03/TTPDCCO-Management-
        Report-2017.pdf

– 2017b. "Scoring and Ranking TRCA's Vegetation
        Communities, Flora, and Fauna Species."
        Toronto: TRCA. January 29, 2020. https://
        s3-ca-central-1.amazonaws.com/trcaca/app/
        uploads/2019/08/21092956/Scoring-and-
        Ranking-Protocol-Final.pdf

– 2020a. "Education and School Field Trips." https://
        tommythompsonpark.ca/education/

– 2020b. "Tommy Thompson Park: Toronto's Urban
        Wilderness." https://www.tommythompsonpark.ca

– 2020c. "Tommy Thompson Park Bird Research Station."
        http://www.ttpbrs.ca

University of Guelph Land Research Group. 2002. *Tommy
        Thompson Park Master Plan Design Projects*.
        Guelph, ON: University of Guelph Land Research
        Group.

Weller, Milton W. 1999. *Wetland Birds: Habitat Resources
        and Conservation Implications*. Cambridge:
        Cambridge University Press.

Wilson, Edward O. 1986. *Biophilia*. Cambridge, MA: Harvard
        University Press.

Abbey, Edward. 1968. *Desert Solitaire*. Tucson: University of Arizona Press.

Aberley, Doug, ed. 1994. *Futures by Design: The Practice of Ecological Planning*. Gabriola Island, BC: New Society Publishers.

Berry, Thomas. 1988. *The Dream of the Earth*. San Francisco: Sierra Club Books.

Bird Life International. https://www.birdlife.org

Brown, Tom Jr. 1993. *Grandfather: A Native American's Lifelong Search for Truth and Harmony with Nature*. New York: Berkley Books

– 1994. *Awakening Spirits: A Native American Path to Inner Peace, Healing, and Spiritual Growth*. New York: Berkley Books.

Burley, Robert. 2017. *An Enduring Wilderness: Toronto's Natural Parklands*. Toronto: ECW Press.

Del Tredici, Peter. 2010. *Wild Urban Plants of the Northeast*. New York: Cornell University Press.

– 2020. *Wild Urban Plants of the Northeast*, 2nd edition. New York: Cornell University Press.

eBird Canada. https://ebird.org/canada/hotspots

Fairburn, M. Jane. *Along the Shore: Rediscovering Toronto's Waterfront Heritage*. Toronto: ECW Press.

Frost, Robert. 1949. *The Complete Poetry of Robert Frost*. Edited by Edward Connery Lathem. New York: Holt, Rinehart & Winston.

Fulford, Robert. 1995. *Accidental City: The Transformation of Toronto*. Toronto: MacFarlane, Walter & Ross.

Gibson, Sally. 1984. *More Than an Island: The History of the Toronto Island*. Toronto: Irwin Publishing.

Grady, Wayne. 1995. *Toronto the Wild: Field Notes of an Urban Naturalist*. Toronto: Macfarlane, Walter & Ross.

Greenburg, Ken. 2019. *Toronto Reborn*. Hamilton, ON: Dundurn Press.

Hewson, Mitchell. 1994. *Horticulture as Therapy*. Guelph, ON: Homewood Health Centre.

Kaplan, Rachel, and Stephen Kaplan. 1989. *The Experience of Nature: A Psychological Perspective*. Cambridge: Cambridge University Press.

Kellert, Steven R., and Edward O. Wilson, eds. 1993. *The Biophilia Hypothesis*. Washington, D.C.: Island Press.

Kinsky, Esther. 2016. *River*. Translated by Iain Galbraith. London: Fitzcarraldo Editions.

Laforme, Chief R. Stacey. 2017. *Living in the Tall Grass: Poems of Reconciliation*. Calgary, AB: Durvile Publications and UpRoute Books and Media.

Leopold, Aldo. 1949. *A Sand Country Almanac*. New York: Oxford University Press.

Li, Qing. 2018. *Forest Bathing: How Trees Can Help You Find Health and Happiness*. New York: Viking Press.

Lopez, Barry. 2019. *Horizon*. Toronto: Random House Canada.

Lopez, Barry Holstun. 1975. *Winter Count*. New York: Scribner.

– 1976. *Desert Notes: Reflections in the Eye of the Raven*. Kansas City, MO: Sheed, Andrews & McMeel.

– 1979. *Rivernotes: The Dance of the Herons*. Kansas City, MO: Andrews McMeel Publishing.

Macfarlane, Robert. 2008. *The Wild Places*. New York: Penguin Books.

– 2012. *The Old Ways: A Journey on Foot*. London: Hamish Hamilton.

– 2015. *Landmarks*. London: Penguin Books.

– 2019. *Underland: A Deep Time Journey*. London: Hamish Hamilton.

Odum, Eugene P. 1975. *Ecology*. New York: Holt, Rinehart & Winston.

Ontario Field Ornithologists. http://ofo.ca

Reed, Peter, and David Rothenberg, eds. 1992. *Wisdom in the Open Air: The Norwegian Roots of Deep Ecology*. Minneapolis: University of Minnesota.

Riley, John L. 2013. *The Once and Future Great Lakes Country: An Ecological Country*. Kingston, ON: McGill-Queen's University Press.

Roszak, Theodore. 1995. *Ecopsychology*. San Francisco: Sierra Club Books.

Roth, Joseph. 2003. *What I Saw: Reports from Berlin, 1920–1930*. Translated by Michael Hofmann. New York: W.W. Norton and Company.

Sauriol, Charles. 1984. *Tales of the Don*. Toronto: Natural Heritage Natural History.

Solnit, Rebecca. 2000. *Wanderlust: A History of Walking*. New York: Viking Penguin.

Stegner, Wallace. 1987. *Crossing to Safety*. New York: Random House.

Sullivan, Louis H. 1990. *A System of Architectural Ornament*. New York: Rizzoli.

Toronto Field Naturalists (TFN). https://torontofieldnaturalists.org

Toronto Ornithological Club. http://torontobirding.ca

Wilson, Edward O. 1978. *On Human Nature*. Cambridge, MA: Harvard University Press.

– 1986. *Biophilia*. Cambridge, MA: Harvard University Press.

Wilson, W.G., and E.D. Cheskey. 2001. *Leslie Street Spit – Tommy Thompson Park Important Bird Area Conservation Plan*. Toronto: Canadian Nature Federation, Bird Studies Canada, and Federation of Ontario Naturalists.

Wohlleben, Peter. 2015. *The Hidden Life of Trees: What They Feel, How They Communicate – Discoveries from a Secret World*. Translated by Jane Billinghurst. Vancouver: Greystone Books.

– 2017. *The Secret Wisdom of Nature: Trees, Animals, and the Extraordinary Balance of All Living Things – Stories from Science and Observation*. Translated by Jane Billinghurst. Vancouver: Greystone Books.

IMAGE KEY

for Robert Burley's photographs

A	Shoreline of the Endikement, 2019	cover
B	Shoreline of Lighthouse Point, 2019	p. ii
C	Wild flowers and grasses on the tip of the Endikement, 2019	p. iv–v
D	The Unassumed Road on the Endikement, 2019	p. vi
E	Submerged hydro pole on the shoreline of the Endikement, 2019	p. viii

Portfolio I

1	View of Lake Ontario from the Endikement, 2019	p. 7
2	Shoreline of the Flats with brick and rebar constructions, 2020	p. 9
3	Cyclists on the shoreline of the Endikement, 2019	p. 11
4	Brick and concrete building remnants, the Endikement, 2020	p. 12
5	Constructions of brick and rebar, Lighthouse Point, 2019	p. 13
6	Cottonwood tree in rubble landform on the Endikement, 2019	p. 14
7	Quaking Aspen trees with metal parts, the Endikement, 2019	p. 15
8	Hawthorn tree on the tip of the Endikement, 2020	p. 17 and back cover
9	Wildflowers in the Flats, 2014	p. 19
10	Landform in the Toplands, 2020	p. 20–21
11	Meadow in the Toplands, 2020	p. 22
12	View of Toronto skyline from Lighthouse Point, 2019	p. 23
13	Lighthouse Point, 2020	p. 24–25
14	Jogger at Cell 3, 2014	p. 26–27
F	Dogwood on the shoreline of the Toplands, 2020	p. 30
G	Birders in the Baselands, 2014	p. 48

Portfolio II

15	The Swing Bridge, Cell 3, the Endikement and Lake Ontario, 2019	p. 56–57
16	Cell 3, 2014	p. 59
17	Fishing at Cell 1, 2013	p. 60–61
18	The Outer Harbour from Peninsula D, 2020	p. 62
19	Triangle Pond, 2020	p. 63
20	Footpath on Peninsula D, 2019	p. 65
21	View of the Toronto skyline from Embayment B, 2019	p. 66
22	View of the Toronto skyline from Embayment A, 2020	p. 67
23	Black-Crowned Night Herons, Embayment D, 2019	p. 68
24	Cormorant nesting area, Peninsula A, 2020	p. 69
25	Aquatic Park Yacht Club, 2019	p. 70
26	The Sunken Woods, 2020	p. 71
27	Willow tree in floodplain, Peninsula A, 2020	p. 73
28	Footbridge in the Wetlands, 2019	p. 74–75
29	The Wetlands, Cell 2, 2020	p. 77
30	Wooded area in Peninsula A, 2014	p. 79
31	The Toronto skyline from Embayment C, 2020	p. 80–81
H	Wild strawberries and lichen, Peninsula D, 2019	p. 98
	Blue Jay, Royal Ontario Museum, Ornithology Collection, 2020	p. 108
	Detail of a Walleyed Pike, 2020	p. 114
I	Cell 1, 2020	p. 118

Portfolio III

32	Entrance to the Unassumed Road, the Neck, 2012	p. 125
33	Landform in the Baselands, 2019	p. 126–27
34	Ice formations on rebar, the Neck, 2019	p. 128
35	Black Willow tree, the Neck, 2019	p. 129
36	Cottonwood tree in concrete rubble, the Neck, 2020	p. 130
37	Cottonwood tree in winter, the Neck, 2020	p. 131
38	Russian olive tree, the Baselands, 2020	p. 133
39	Hydro poles on the shoreline of the Neck, 2019	p. 134
40	Garlic Mustard, the Neck, 2020	p. 135
41	Woodland thicket, the Baselands, 2020	p. 137
42	Wildflowers, the Baselands, 2019	p. 138
43	The Hearn Generating Station, the Baselands, 2019	p. 139
44	Footpath at the entrance, the Neck, 2020	p. 140–41
45	Black Willow tree, the Baselands, 2020	p. 142
46	Concrete rubble and tire, the Baselands, 2019	p. 143
47	Chain link fences at the entrance to the Endikement, 2020	p. 145
48	Visitor Centre, the Neck, 2020	p. 146
49	Defunct truck entrance and maintenance yard, the Neck, 2020	p. 147
50	Corner of Leslie Street and Unwin Avenue as seen from the park entrance, 2020	p. 148–49
J	Table construction on Peninsula A, 2020	p. 152
K	Shoreline of the Neck, 2012	p. 160

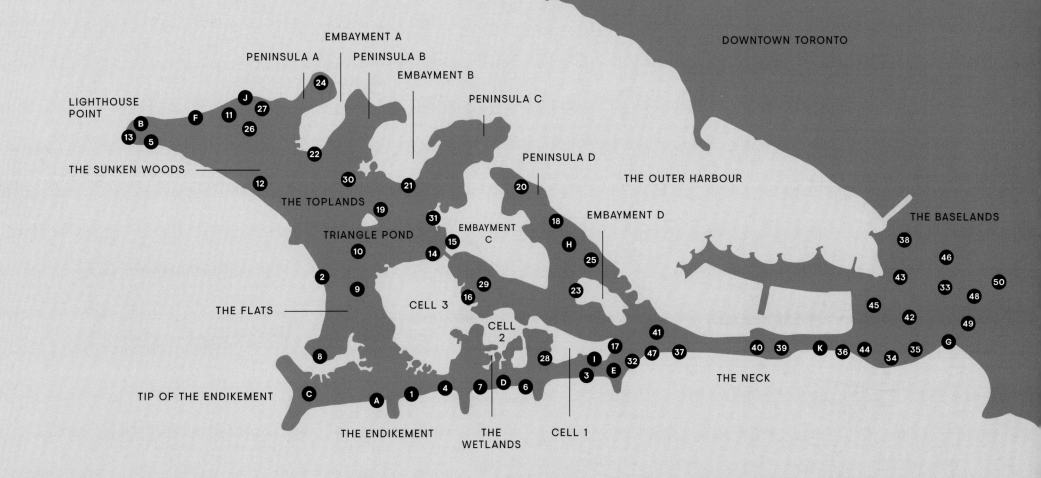

DOWNTOWN TORONTO

EMBAYMENT A

PENINSULA A   PENINSULA B

EMBAYMENT B

LIGHTHOUSE
POINT   PENINSULA C

THE SUNKEN WOODS   PENINSULA D

THE OUTER HARBOUR

THE TOPLANDS   EMBAYMENT D   THE BASELANDS

Triangle Pond   EMBAYMENT
C

THE FLATS   CELL 3

CELL
2

TIP OF THE ENDIKEMENT   THE NECK

THE ENDIKEMENT   THE   CELL 1
                     WETLANDS

LAKE ONTARIO

This map highlights the
locations of photographs
by Robert Burley.

TOMMY THOMPSON PARK

CONTRIBUTORS

WALTER H. KEHM

Walter H. Kehm developed his passion for landscape through bird watching in the wetlands surrounding JFK Airport in New York. He is a landscape architect, retired professor, and former director of the School of Landscape Architecture at the University of Guelph. He has an international practice and taught at many architecture and landscape architecture programs around the globe. His recent projects include the award-winning Trillium Park at Ontario Place in Toronto.

ROBERT BURLEY

Robert Burley is a photographer whose work often explores the transition between city and country. He has completed a number of long-term projects that investigate the presence of nature in an urban setting. His photographs have been widely exhibited and can be found in museum collections around the globe. Robert lives in Toronto with his family, teaches at Ryerson University's School of Image Arts, and is represented by the Stephen Bulger Gallery.

JOHN CARLEY

Since 1986, John Carley has been co-chair of Friends of the Spit, a citizen advocacy group established in 1977, dedicated to preserving the Leslie Street Spit and Baselands as a public urban wilderness for recreational enjoyment. In addition to his advocacy for the Spit, in 1995 John initiated the Toronto Butterfly Count, a continuing annual census. As an architect and birder, John was a volunteer member of the City of Toronto Bird-Friendly Development Working Group since 2011.

ANDREA CHRESTON

Andrea Chreston is the Project Manager of Tommy Thompson Park with Toronto and Region Conservation Authority (TRCA). Andrea has been a proud member of the team that has helped shape this incredible urban wilderness since 2007. She holds a BSc (Env) from the University of Guelph and is passionate about restoring habitat for wildlife and improving the natural world.

PETER DEL TREDICI

Peter Del Tredici is a botanist specializing in the growth and development of trees. He worked at the Arnold Arboretum of Harvard University for 35 years and has taught at both the Harvard Graduate School of Design and MIT. His interests are wide ranging and include the ecology and taxonomy of hemlocks and the history of the ginkgo tree. His recent work is focused on urban ecology and climate change, and he just published the second edition of the widely acclaimed *Wild Urban Plants of the Northeast: A Field Guide* (Cornell University Press 2020).

CHIEF R. STACEY LAFORME

R. Stacey Laforme is the elected Chief of the Mississaugas of the New Credit First Nation (MNCFN). Born and raised on MNCFN, Chief Laforme has served his community since 1999. Chief Laforme is committed to the increased involvement and communication between Elected Council and both on- and off-reserve membership. He is very active throughout MNCFN's traditional territory, which encompasses 3.9 million acres of Southern Ontario, not only as a Chief but as a notable storyteller and poet. Chief Laforme has been appointed an honorary senior fellow for Massey College and was also recently recognized with the Walter Cooke Wisdom Keeper Award by the De dwa da dehs nye>s (Aboriginal Health Centre).

GORD MACPHERSON

Gord MacPherson was a fish and wildlife technician with the Toronto and Region Conservation Authority (TRCA), responsible for the development and management of Tommy Thompson Park. During his career at TRCA, Gord was responsible for broad-based Environmental Monitoring Programs and pioneered Conservation/Stewardship Outreach programs, as well as Habitat Restoration Projects. He was awarded the A.D. Latornell Conservation Leadership Award for his contribution to conservation in the Province of Ontario.

DAVID MILLER

David Miller is the Director of International Diplomacy and Global Ambassador of Inclusive Climate Action at C40 Cities Climate Leadership Group, where he is responsible for supporting nearly 100 mayors of the world's largest cities in their climate leadership and building a global movement for socially equitable action to mitigate and adapt to climate change. During his two terms as Mayor of Toronto from 2003 to 2010, the city became internationally known for its environmental initiatives, economic strength, and social integration. Miller is a Harvard-trained economist and professionally a lawyer.

GAVIN MILLER

Gavin Miller has been a flora biologist with Toronto and Region Conservation Authority (TRCA) for 20 years. He conducts regular inventories of natural areas and manages data records for almost 1,900 plant species that occur or have occurred within the jurisdiction. He has a master's in environmental studies from York University and has been observing the natural areas in the Toronto area (including Tommy Thompson Park) since childhood.

WAYNE REEVES

Wayne Reeves is Chief Curator for City of Toronto Museums & Heritage Services. He is also a widely published historical geographer who has focused on the interplay between nature and culture in Toronto, including the establishment and evolution of the city's public greenspaces. He contributed essays to numerous books and was co-editor of *HTO: Toronto's Water from Lake Iroquois to Lost Rivers to Low-flow Toilets*.

GARTH VERNON RILEY

Garth Vernon Riley is a co-chair of Friends of the Spit and as such has provided valuable input as a consultant on a variety of naturalization and re-naturalization projects in Toronto. He is also the eBird Reviewer for Toronto. He obtained a BSc (Biology) from the University of Guelph in 1977 and in 1980 began a career with the Ontario Public Health Laboratory as a medical laboratory technologist in microbiology. He retired from the Ontario Agency for Health Protection and Promotion as Director of the Toronto Public Health Laboratory in 2013.